MW00614622

EVALUATING
INSTRUCTIONAL
COACHING

SHARON
THOMAS

JIM
KNIGHT

MICHELLE
HARRIS

ANN
HOFFMAN

EVALUATING INSTRUCTIONAL COACHING

PEOPLE,
PROGRAMS,
AND PARTNERSHIP

SUSTAINING
COACHING
PROGRAMS

HIRING
INSTRUCTIONAL
COACHES

EVALUATING
COACHING
PROGRAMS

EVALUATING
INSTRUCTIONAL
COACHES

WHY
EVALUATION
MATTERS

ONE FINE BIRD / PRESS

Lawrence, Kansas USA

ascd

Alexandria, Virginia USA

1703 N. Beauregard St. • Alexandria, VA 22311-1714 USA
Phone: 800-933-2723 or 703-578-9600 • Fax: 703-575-5400
Website: www.ascd.org • Email: member@ascd.org
Author guidelines: www.ascd.org/write

Ranjit Sidhu, *CEO & Executive Director;* Penny Reinart, *Chief Impact Officer;* Genny Ostertag, *Senior Director, Acquisitions & Editing;* Susan Hills, *Senior Acquisitions Editor;* Julie Houtz, *Director, Book Editing;* Megan Doyle, *Editor;* Thomas Lytle, *Creative Director;* Donald Ely, *Art Director;* Georgia Park, *Senior Graphic Designer;* Valerie Younkin, *Senior Production Designer;* Kelly Marshall, *Production Manager;* Shajuan Martin, *E-Publishing Specialist;* Christopher Logan, *Senior Production Specialist*

ONE FINE BIRD /PRESS

853 N. 1663 Road
Lawrence KS 66049
Phone: 308-496-4724 • E-mail: hello@instructionalcoaching.com
Website: www.instructionalcoaching.com

Edited by Kirsten McBride and Sharon Thomas
Cover Design by Chase Christensen
Interior Design by Chase Christensen and Mycaela Erben

Copyright © 2022 Instructional Coaching Group. All rights reserved. It is illegal to reproduce copies of this work in print or electronic format (including reproductions displayed on a secure intranet or stored in a retrieval system or other electronic storage device from which copies can be made or displayed) without the prior written permission of the publisher. By purchasing only authorized electronic or print editions and not participating in or encouraging piracy of copyrighted materials, you support the rights of authors and publishers. Readers who wish to reproduce or republish excerpts of this work in print or electronic format may do so for a small fee by contacting the Copyright Clearance Center (CCC), 222 Rosewood Dr., Danvers, MA 01923, USA (phone: 978-750-8400; fax: 978-646-8600; web: www.copyright.com). To inquire about site licensing options or any other reuse, contact ASCD Permissions at www.ascd.org/permissions or permission@ascd.org. For a list of vendors authorized to license ASCD e-books to institutions, see www.ascd.org/epubs. Send translation inquiries to translations@ascd.org.

ASCD® is a registered trademark of Association for Supervision and Curriculum Development. All other trademarks contained in this book are the property of, and reserved by, their respective owners, and are used for editorial and informational purposes only. No such use should be construed to imply sponsorship or endorsement of the book by the respective owners.

All web links in this book are correct as of the publication date below but may have become inactive or otherwise modified since that time. If you notice a deactivated or changed link, please email books@ascd.org with the words "Link Update" in the subject line. In your message, please specify the web link, the book title, and the page number on which the link appears.

PAPERBACK ISBN: 978-1-4166-3084-5   ASCD product #122039   n10/21

PDF E-BOOK ISBN: 978-1-4166-3085-2   See Books in Print for other formats.

Quantity discounts are available: email programteam@ascd.org or call 800-933-2723, ext. 5773, or 703-575-5773. For desk copies, go to www.ascd.org/deskcopy.

Library of Congress Cataloging-in-Publication Data
Names: Thomas, Sharon (English teacher), author. | Knight, Jim, author. | Hoffman, Ann, author. | Harris, Michelle (English teacher), author.
Title: Evaluating instructional coaching : people, programs, and partnership / Sharon Thomas, Jim Knight, Ann Hoffman, Michelle Harris.
Description: Alexandria, Virginia : ASCD, 2021. | Includes bibliographical references and index. |
Identifiers: LCCN 2021023232 (print) | LCCN 2021023233 (ebook) | ISBN 9781416630845 (paperback) | ISBN 9781416630852 (pdf)
Subjects: LCSH: Mentoring in education. | Teachers--In-service training.
Classification: LCC LB1731.4 .T459 2021 (print) | LCC LB1731.4 (ebook) | DDC 371.102--dc23
LC record available at https://lccn.loc.gov/2021023232
LC ebook record available at https://lccn.loc.gov/2021023233

30 29 28 27 26 25 24 23 22 21   1 2 3 4 5 6 7 8 9 10 11 12

TABLE OF CONTENTS

VIII   Preface

XII   Acknowledgments

XVIII   About the Authors

CHAPTER 1

1   **WHY EVALUATION MATTERS**

5   Where We Are

16   Where We Need to Be

19   How We Get to Where We Need to Be

24   Our Hope for This Book

CHAPTER 2

33   **EVALUATING INSTRUCTIONAL COACHES**

37   Research on Coaching That Moves Students

50   Connecting What the Coach Does to What Students Do

CHAPTER 3

85   **EVALUATING INSTRUCTIONAL COACHING PROGRAMS**

90   Measuring Success at the Program Level

114   System Responsibility for Coaching Success

CHAPTER 4

127   **RECRUITING AND HIRING INSTRUCTIONAL COACHES**

132   The Hiring Process

151   Recruiting Instructional Coaches

158   Helpful Interview Processes

CHAPTER 5

189   **RETAINING COACHES AND SUSTAINING COACHING PROGRAMS**

195   Retaining Instructional Coaches

208   Sustaining Instructional Coaching Programs

222   References

230   Appendices

291   Index

DEDICATED TO

We dedicate this book to all of the educators who

have endured a painful, inaccurate, insulting evalu-

ation process that made you question why you ever

became an educator.

PREFACE

_____

Recently I wrote about two different models of

professional development: outside in and inside

out. Using outside-in professional development,

leaders identify an important, usually evidence-

based, teaching strategy and then provide training

to teachers with the expectation that they will learn

the strategy and implement it. The thinking behind

this approach makes sense. Research has been

done, and the new strategy has been found to be

powerful, so teachers should implement it. But from

the teachers' perspective, with the outside-in model,

learning is forced on teachers. It is not surprising,

therefore, that outside-in professional development

is often unsuccessful.

The outside-in model is grounded in the assumption that specific strategies will be useful in all classrooms, and that all teachers, therefore, should implement them, whether they like them or not. When teachers explain that a strategy they're being taught isn't a good fit for their way of teaching or helpful for their students for some reason, they are often considered resistant. Additionally, most people are not motivated by other people's goals for them in all contexts, so teachers often passively resist outside-in training, repeating the widely used phrase, "This too shall pass." And, of course, they are often right. A professional development model that ignores teacher voice and minimizes teacher autonomy likely isn't structured for success and won't lead to high-quality implementation. Eventually, the new strategy will likely be dropped.

An alternative is inside-out professional development. This model begins with the experiences of students and teachers in their classrooms. That is, in a variety of ways, teachers start by getting a clear picture of how students are learning and experiencing a class and how they are teaching. Then, they set a goal that they really want to hit because they can see it will have an unmistakably positive impact on their students. Following this, they identify a strategy they will use to try and hit the goal. Finally, they adapt the goal, sometimes drop it for another goal, and keep making adjustments until they hit the goal. With the inside-out model, real learning happens in real life.

The problem with inside-out learning, though, is that it takes time. Teachers need to find a way to get a clear picture of reality, do the research to identify a strategy, figure out how to implement it, gather data on changes in their students as they implement the strategy, and then think through adaptations. Since teachers are already very busy, adding all of that mental work can be too much. Consequently, teachers are often unable to implement inside-out professional development on their own. What they need is a learning partner to help them. That partner is an instructional coach.

When instructional coaching is done well, coaches help teachers bring inside-out learning to life. But the key here is: Coaching has to be done well. After studying instructional coaching for more than two decades, we have found that seven success factors are essential for coaches to be successful. The seven factors are as follows (Knight, 2021):

1. **A WAY OF BEING**: Coaches need a set of principles to guide their actions so that their actions encourage partnership rather than engender resistance. We refer to these as the Partnership Principles.

2. **A PROCESS**: Coaches need to have a conversational framework that they can use to move through the stages of a coaching cycle, addressing such issues as getting a clear picture of reality, setting goals, identifying and learning strategies for hitting the goal, gathering data, and making adaptions until the goal is hit. We refer to this as the Impact Cycle.

3. **DATA**: Coaches need to know how to gather engagement and achievement data so that they can partner with teachers as teachers set goals and measure progress toward them.

4. **TEACHING STRATEGIES**: Once goals are set, coaches need to have a deep understanding of teaching strategies they can suggest to teachers to help them hit their goals.

5. **COMMUNICATION HABITS AND SKILLS**: Coaches need to ask effective, powerful questions, listen with empathy, build connections, share positive information effectively, and use other sound communication habits and skills.

6. **LEADERSHIP**: Coaches need to lead themselves effectively, manage their time, develop healthy habits, use self-care, and

lead others effectively by being multipliers, understanding and addressing school culture, and aligning themselves with colleagues.

7. **SYSTEM SUPPORT:** Coaches need system support. The preceding six factors will have little impact if coaches don't work in systems that support them—where their role is clear, they have time to implement the Impact Cycle, policies about confidentiality are understood and followed, and school leaders act in ways that support coaches.

Instructional coaches, then, need to become proficient in new beliefs, processes, skills, and knowledge, and the settings in which they work need to value and support where their efforts. To accomplish this, districts need to provide significant professional development support based on the inside-out model with coaches having their own coaches, often referred to as coaching champions. Additionally, they need standards and tools to clarify how well coaches and systems are progressing in their movement toward proficient implementation of all seven factors. This book provides those tools. We intend it to be a GPS for powerful coaching.

Coaching, as we describe it, is a form of professional development that honors teachers' professionalism. We don't believe you can bully teachers into becoming reflective professionals. The same holds true for coaches. The best kind of evaluation fosters growth by celebrating the ability to think for oneself. That is our goal with this book. When coaches' professionalism is respected, they, in turn, will respect the professionalism of teachers. And when teachers' professionalism is honored, everyone benefits, especially students.

— Jim Knight

ACKNOWLEDGMENTS

FROM THE AUTHORS

The Instructional Couching Group (ICG) instructional coaching program audit described in chapter 3 would not have been possible without the collaboration of Katy Independent School District (ISD) in Katy, TX. When the Katy ISD leadership team sought to evaluate their 11-year-old coaching program, they reached out to ICG. In partnership, we were able to create a process customized to fit their district. Our many discussions and the questions they posed throughout this audit process significantly influenced our thinking as we refined our processes around program evaluation. Our gratitude goes to the exceptional leadership team of Dr. Christine Caskey, Dr. Kim Lawson, Dr. Cazilda Steele, Dr. Annie Wolf, Jackie Zimmerman, and Marlene Portier. We are eternally grateful for their time, effort, and expertise.

We sought out the input of two school-based human resources professionals to ensure that this book is sound not only from a coaching perspective but also from a human resources perspective as well. Sue Robertson, Chief Human Resource Officer, Beaverton (OR) School District, and Aretha Young, Certification Team Leader, Harford County (MD) Public Schools, helped us to understand some of the day-to-day realities that can influence a district's ability to implement some of our suggestions so that the we could incorporate those challenges. Seeking out the input of human resources professionals is not just important for managers who hire instructional coaches but for us as well.

In addition, some of our long-term partners allowed us to examine their instructional coach job descriptions as part of our research for this book: Rantoul (IL) Township High School, Lansing (MI) Public Schools, Fairfax County (VA) Public Schools, and California Virtual Academies. Their willingness to share these materials expanded our thinking about the hiring process, and we thank them for their ongoing collaboration and commitment to instructional coaching. Michelle Lis at Fairfax County Public Schools also provided us with her district's coach evaluation rubric, which helped us to think more deeply about our own. The collegiality of these partners is an enormous part of our own continuous improvement.

We also thank Mark Dowley at Brighton Grammar School in Brighton, Victoria, Australia, for his interview with Jim, which provided us with important new thinking about applying the Kirkpatrick Four-Level Training Evaluation Model to instructional coaching.

Finally, we cannot say enough about our wonderful ICG staff, including Jennifer Ryschon Knight, Emily Malatesta, Erin Krownapple, Chase Christensen, Sasha Strunk, Ruth Ryschon, Brooke Deaton, Geoff Knight, and Matthew Kelly, who support us all with humor and grace. Their dedication is without question. We are grateful and honored to work with them every day.

FROM SHARON THOMAS

I was fortunate to have excellent school- and district-based administrators who helped me to navigate teacher and instructional coach evaluation over the years. Principals Dr. D'Ette Devine, Vincent Cariello, Wesley Zimmerman, Kathleen Kist, and Dr. David Foye strove to make evaluation processes fair and helpful and to make evaluation conversations ones in which I felt safe, encouraged to use my voice, engaged, and open to new ideas. I entered the writing of this book mostly with trepidation but also a little bit of hope because of their work in showing me that good evaluation is an ongoing process.

At ICG, I am fortunate to work with Jim Knight, Ann Hoffman, and Michelle Harris, who continue to encourage my growth in understanding how to support educators and schools and to show me patience and friendship along the way.

Finally, my personal support team has had quite a year, as we all have. My closest friends of many decades, Sandy Bracy and Jennifer Jones, are there for me in every way, in both crisis and celebration. Sandy, my sister, Lauren Bass, and all of my teacher friends remind me of the selfless commitment of teachers in classrooms every single day, even when—especially when—they are asked to work in ways that no teacher ever has before. And my husband, Randy Cover, is simply a gem of a human. He helped our writing team with resources for this book because of his project management and human resources background all the while navigating my occasional writing meltdowns as well. I wouldn't get anything done, including this book, without him.

FROM JIM KNIGHT

This book, like every book I have written, wouldn't be possible without the support of my life partner, Jenny, whose profound and unwavering support has helped me write every word I put down on every page. My sons and daughter, now all making their own beautiful ruckuses in the world, inspire and encourage me, and give me hope that a brighter future is possible. A world filled with people like them will be a better world. Geoff, Cam, Dave, Emily, Ben, Isaiah, and Luke, I love you, and I'm grateful for your patience with me as I do my best to make my way forward.

FROM ANN HOFFMAN

I have had the great fortune to be mentored by outstanding individuals over my many years in education. Dr. Jim Knight and Dr. Don Deshler at the University of Kansas are at the top of that list. I am humbled by the generosity of these great educators. They have always taken the time to honor my voice, encourage my thinking, and support my efforts. Their work and passion have been my guide and my inspiration. I am grateful that they have entrusted me to share their work.

As for my ICG colleagues and friends, Michelle Harris and Sharon Thomas, I could not ask for more. They are both extraordinary. I am in awe of their knowledge, generosity, and never-ending support and collaboration. Partnering with them has deepened my knowledge and expanded my perspectives. Additionally, they have been both my sounding board and my cheerleader. I am so grateful.

To my many school partners, how fortunate I am to work with such outstanding educators. It is an honor and a privilege to partner with and learn from all of them. I am inspired by their work, and I can never thank them enough for their willingness and generosity of time to reflect, experiment, and learn and laugh together. I am in awe of their unwavering dedication to creating a better world for students and teachers.

Last, the love of my life, my spouse, Jim (my "other" Jim). His encouragement, love, and support never waiver. He keeps me grounded and focused on the important things in life. He is my best friend and biggest cheerleader. He has made my career possible, and he inspires me every day.

FROM MICHELLE HARRIS

From the time I was a teacher, through serving an instructional coach, and then into my years as an administrator, I fought the urge to make evaluation a once-a-year feat. It made so much more sense to me to make it something I understood and constantly returned to in the reflective moments of my teaching, my coaching, and, then, as an "evaluator," others' teaching. I am so grateful for the many mentors who furthered my understanding of how a good evaluation tool is both an assessment and a driving force for planning and delivering excellent instruction and how good evaluation works from the cornerstone concept of "we can *all* get better." In Beaverton, Oregon, where I served students for 17 years, Sue Robertson, principal and human resources extraordinaire, Jill O'Neill, my brilliant colleague and mentor, and Shirley Brock, my hilarious and equally brilliant friend and mentor, all helped me immensely along this path. They answered my questions, nudged me when things got tough, and partnered with me to use evaluation to do best by students. I owe them a huge debt of gratitude.

At ICG, there aren't enough words to express my gratitude for those with whom I work. Jim Knight, Sharon Thomas, and Ann Hoffman push my thinking, encourage my growth, and laugh heartily with me, besides being true and real friends.

Finally, in a year full of craziness, I owe my sanity and health to my husband, Dave, who, in typical fashion, has handled it all with the calm grace that is quintessentially Dave. Our boys, Porter and Finlay, have missed milestone events (16th birthdays, drivers' license celebrations, first years of high school, hanging out with friends, not to mention sports ... sports ... and more sports) and have handled it all with as much grace and humor as teenagers possibly can. This family of mine is absolutely the only reason I can do what I do. They support me and buoy me up every single step of the way. Thanks, boys. I love you.

ABOUT THE AUTHORS

———

Sharon Thomas, senior consultant at ICG, is a National Board Certified English teacher, instructional coach, student advocate, and writer. She was a teacher and instructional coach in public schools for nearly two decades. Along with her work in ICG workshops and books, Sharon developed the ICG Coaching Certification process. She is also a consultant for the Touchstones Discussion Project and a certified SIM Professional Developer in the area of writing. She is the founder of the Cecil County [Maryland] Teacher Leadership Network and has presented at conferences across North America on instructional coaching, professional learning, secondary school literacy, and teacher leadership. Her experience with teacher leadership in school reform was published in *Principal Leadership*, and she is a coauthor of *The Instructional Playbook* (Knight et al., 2020). Sharon lives in Baltimore, Maryland, with her husband.

Jim Knight, senior partner at ICG, has spent more than two decades studying professional learning, effective teaching, and instructional coaching. He is a founding senior partner of ICG and a senior research associate at the University of Kansas Center for Research on Learning (KU-CRL). Jim's book *Instructional Coaching: A Partnership Approach to Improving Instruction* (Knight, 2007) was the first comprehensive book focused on instructional coaching; similarly Jim's book *Focus on Teaching* (Knight, 2014) was the first book-length publication addressing the topic of video and professional development. Jim's other books include *Unmistakable Impact* (Knight, 2011), *High-Impact Instruction* (Knight, 2013), *Better Conversations* (Knight, 2016), *The Impact Cycle* (Knight, 2017), and *The Instructional Playbook* (Knight et al., 2020).

Jim's articles on professional learning, teaching, and instructional coaching have appeared in journals such as *The Journal of Staff*

Development, Principal Leadership, The School Administrator, Kappan, and *Educational Leadership.* Frequently asked to lead professional learning, Jim has presented to more than 100,000 educators from six continents. He has a PhD in Education from the University of Kansas and has won several university teaching, innovation, and service awards. Jim also created the Radical Learners blog.

Ann Hoffman, senior consultant at ICG, and a professional development leader for the University of Kansas Center for Research on Learning (KU-CRL), has more than 30 years of experience in the field. As one of the first professional developers for KU-CRL as well as one of the first consultants with ICG, Ann has worked with thousands of teachers, coaches, and administrators in the United States and internationally. Ann is a recipient of the Gordon R. Alley Partnership Award and the Strategic Instruction Model Leadership Award, both from KU-CRL. She is also the 2017 recipient of the Don Deshler Leadership Award from ICG, and she is a co-author of *The Instructional Playbook* (2020). In addition, Ann serves as a founding member of the advisory board for the Belin-Blank Center for Gifted and Talented Education at the University of Iowa. Ann lives in Iowa and California with her family.

Michelle Harris, senior consultant at ICG, began teaching in El Cajon, California. She taught middle school English and social studies before serving as an instructional coach, Title I coordinator, student manager, and assistant principal at three middle schools, a K-8 school, and a 6-12 IBO school, all in Beaverton, Oregon. A seasoned staff developer, Michelle has presented and keynoted all over the United States and in Europe and Africa, and she is a co-author of *The Instructional Playbook* (2020). She lives in Portland, Oregon, with her husband and two sons. When not working, she enjoys reading, traveling, attending her sons' numerous sporting events, entertaining friends and family, and sitting in a chair on a sunny beach.

CHAPTER 1

WHY EVALUATION MATTERS

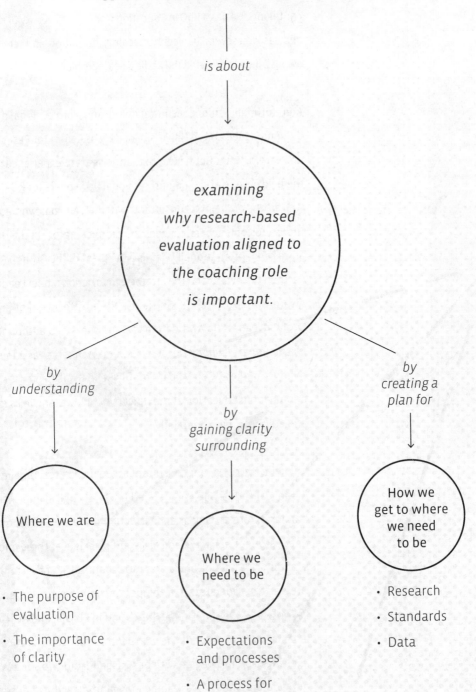

is about

*examining
why research-based
evaluation aligned to
the coaching role
is important.*

*by
understanding*

*by
gaining clarity
surrounding*

*by
creating a
plan for*

Where we are

Where we
need to be

How we
get to where
we need
to be

- The purpose of evaluation
- The importance of clarity

- Expectations and processes
- A process for improvement

- Research
- Standards
- Data

01

WHY EVALUATION
MATTERS

 **SNAPSHOT:**

This chapter describes challenges facing school

districts when evaluating instructional coaches and

coaching programs. It outlines the book's approach

to evaluation and the thinking behind it. You can skip

this chapter if you already know you need changes

in your evaluation system and want specifics on

how to do that.

Standards. Assessment. Evaluation. Accountability.
**As a high school teacher and instructional coach,
Malikah has applied these terms to both students
and herself many times over.**

As a teacher, she welcomed the Standards Movement of the 1990s
in her early teaching years to address content accountability. After
all, was it really such a stretch that teachers and schools should
have some way to specify which concepts students should learn in
which grades? In Malikah's student teaching experience, when she
was given free rein to teach whatever she wanted to ninth graders,
she wished she had more guidance. "Have they already learned
the parts of a sentence? A paragraph? An essay? Have they read
Shakespeare before? How do we know?" The Standards Movement
promised to answer the fundamental questions of "What *should*
they know?" and "What *do* they know?" and allowed states to tailor
standards and their assessments to their own needs and priorities.
Malikah had faith that her state would work it out.

When the No Child Left Behind Act (NCLB, 2001) came along, she
thought that made sense, too. For too long, the inconsistent
quality of public education from state to state and district to
district (and the extraordinary equity issues that ensued) had
alarmed educators and frustrated families. National oversight
made sense. Consequences for poor performance made sense.
Malikah had faith that the federal government would work it out.

Later, when NCLB's approach to school improvement exposed problems in the notion of punishing schools who most need support, the federal Race to the Top (U.S. Department of Education, 2009) competitive grant program entered the fray. Variations in the rigorousness of state standards and testing programs under NCLB had everyone wondering whose state programs were best: "How do our kids *really* stack up? Are we assessing the right things?" The idea of consistency across states made sense. This time, the rules promised less punishment and more support when students performed poorly. They also promised more individual teacher accountability for school improvement and more fairness, relevance, and specificity in teacher evaluation. Although Malikah had less faith that the government would work it out after what happened with NCLB, still she hoped for the best.

While waiting to see what would happen with national student assessment under Race to the Top, school districts had time to focus on how they would change teacher evaluation. Like so many districts nationwide, Malikah's district decided to use Charlotte Danielson's *Enhancing Professional Practice: A Framework for Teaching* (2007) to design its teacher evaluation system. Yet, her district's version of that framework bore little resemblance to anyone else's because Danielson's work was interpreted in so many different ways across districts nationwide. In fact, sometimes interpretations varied so widely that what made a teacher "needing improvement" in Malikah's district was considered "effective" for a teacher in the next county over.

In Malikah's district, the planning and instruction items from the previous teacher evaluation form now constituted 50% of her overall evaluation, whereas whole-school improvement data and data targets she set for her own students comprised the other half. Every year, the way those data points were calculated changed. Every year, teachers felt that none of those data points accurately assessed their teaching (positively or negatively). Every year, "fairness" seemed elusive. "Accountability" seemed to refer "only to what teachers are doing wrong," not the good work they were doing every day.

When the new national student assessments were released, they, too, were disappointing. They were not as closely aligned to the standards as teachers had expected, and the ways that questions were structured seemed to run counter to research on testing validity and reliability. As a result, many states left the newly established testing consortia and reverted back to their own state tests. Malikah, who had never been allowed to voluntarily exit unfair assessments of her own work, wondered, "States can do that? So what then is a truly good assessment of learning?" Fairness and accountability seemed elusive for students as well.

Amid all of this confusion and inconsistency, amid all of the good intentions and missteps, Malikah and her fellow teachers showed up to school every day and did the best job they could. Knowing that their work would be misunderstood and often inadequately evaluated, they taught their students anyway.

But the previous 20 years did take their toll. Malikah has less confidence in new assessment paradigms for students and for teachers. With every new attempt to improve an evaluation system, she shrugs her shoulders and wonders, "What is it this time?" Malikah has always been a positive force in schools, but even she has become jaded on the subject of evaluation and accountability.

A few years ago, Malikah left the classroom and decided to become an instructional coach. She wants to support teachers through this uncertain maze of school reform. She wants reform to work for teachers—and especially for students—as much as humanly possible. She wants students to get what they need to have the lives they want, and she knows that teachers want that, too. What she didn't know was that her evaluation as an instructional coach in her building (and indeed the whole coaching program in her school district) had no more clarity, alignment, or validity than student or teacher evaluation did. When her principal explained to her that, "Well, we don't have a specific form to evaluate coaches, so we'll just tweak the teacher form a little, OK? We'll figure it out," Malikah's first thought was, "Here we go again."

Where We Are

Accountability is a need in any given school system. Any organization that involves the education, care, and support of children should be held to high standards regarding how those services are delivered. Approximately 80% of school budgets are spent on staffing (National Center for Education Statistics, 2021), so schools must be accountable to taxpayers, school boards, parents, community members and, most important, students. Measuring effectiveness is not possible without continually reflecting on practice and evaluating how practice aligns with actual progress on student outcomes.

We can't begin to count how many times we've been asked by school and school system leaders for help in evaluating the good work their coaches are doing in classrooms. Even though these leaders are beholden to laws and policies regarding employee evaluation, few evaluation systems are specifically geared toward coaching roles. School leaders have an additional layer of accountability with regard to coaching positions because coaches often are released from all classroom teaching duties, and leaders, therefore, must provide justification for these roles. To deal with this issue, some districts use a catch-all evaluation form for "teachers on special assignment" (TOSAs), even though those TOSA roles are often extremely varied and may bear no resemblance to each other. Others take an existing teacher evaluation system and try to modify it to work for coaches, which is about as effective as evaluating how well an apple is performing as an orange, yet that is the most common "coaching evaluation" process we see in schools. Clearly, that process is not helpful to leaders, coaches, or the school itself.

In addition to lacking a clear and helpful process for evaluating coaching positions, school leaders often tell us that no formal evaluation process for overall coaching programs is in place either, a deep concern in an era of near-constant education budget debates. No data on coaching program impact means that coaching programs are constantly on the budgetary chopping block, and cutting coaching positions does not help teachers or students to improve.

From a whole-school perspective, without specific metrics specifying the quality of a program implementation in a targeted area, appropriate evaluation to help guide improvement efforts is extremely challenging. That is, lack of specificity about how the implementation is going makes helpful conversations about improvements or next steps among administrators, coaches, and teachers nearly impossible. Not surprisingly, many reform efforts involve false or exaggerated claims of success (Guskey, 2000). Ensuring that schools and school districts have accurate information about both coaches and coaching programs is crucial to guide both improvement in supporting classrooms and ensuring accountability.

When evaluation processes work best, employees can use that process to set goals for improvement in their work. With sound practices in place to evaluate instructional coaches and coaching programs, instructional coaches will get better in their work, and that means teachers will get better in their work and, ultimately, that students will learn more.

On the other hand, when evaluation processes are not clear or aligned to a set of standards, employees sometimes "check out" because they don't feel seen or appreciated by their supervisors. Malikah learned long ago that her observations and evaluations were merely hurdles to navigate each year, not conversations about her ambitions for her own growth or that of her students. After many years of participating in evaluations that she knew would not substantially change anything, during post-observation conferences, she would smile, nod her head, sign the form, and then head to lunch. Poor evaluation tools that merely go through the motions and "check boxes" unintentionally discourage employees and make setting improvement goals difficult.

Too often, evaluation is viewed as a bookkeeping task that leaders must monitor and not as an improvement process for supporting employees. The uncomfortable nature of one adult telling another adult "how you're doing" at work leads many leaders to want to make the interaction as brief and as mild as possible, regardless of what's happening with the employee.

Jim recalls a principal once explaining his litmus test for successful evaluation conferences: "If the teacher doesn't cry or get angry, then I feel it's a good evaluation." Michelle once worked for a principal who told her that the basis for how positive or negative his teacher evaluations are is whether parents had called to complain. These are very low bars and ones that discourage honest conversations about performance and improvement. When both the evaluator and the employee end the evaluation process primarily feeling relief that it's over, there's a problem.

To advocate for change in the evaluation of coaching and coaching programs, this chapter

» examines the purposes of evaluation processes,
» reinforces the importance of clarity around every facet of job performance,

- » gives an overview of expectations and processes that are key to fostering an evaluation as a process for improvement, and
- » describes some of the research guiding the development of our evaluation rubrics.

THE PURPOSE OF EVALUATION

Periodic evaluations for employees in any job can be useful. According to the Society for Human Resources Management (SHRM; Fleischer, 2018), reasons to evaluate include "providing a rational basis on which to promote, discipline, and terminate" (p. 42). SHRM also advocates for the important evidence that periodic evaluations can provide to ensure that any "adverse actions" that an employer takes involving an employee are not discriminatory or improper, and cites new employees as finding evaluations particularly helpful as they learn the job (p. 42). SHRM cautions, though, that when evaluations do not follow best practices, evaluations can "do more harm than good" (p. 42).

The idea of evaluation itself is not the villain. Evaluation problems can arise from any of several sources:

- » evaluators not using data reliably to inform the evaluation (for coaches, this connects to issues surrounding data not directly tied to coaching, as we discuss in chapter 2),
- » employees not having a clear picture of reality about their performance (for coaches, this connects directly to issues surrounding role clarity, as we discuss in chapters 2 and 4),
- » the defensive response that most professionals have to feedback and advice (for coaches, this connects to the way supervisors often handle coaches' evaluation conversations, as we discuss in chapters 2 and 4), and
- » the tendency of some evaluation tools to oversimplify the complexities of the job (for coaches, the issue of using another role's evaluation form or process looms large here, as we discuss in chapter 2).

Few employees push back on the idea of receiving an evaluation and feedback on their work. It's the way that leaders handle evaluation that employees typically find troubling, especially when they feel that evaluation processes are not aligned with the job they've been asked to do or are not fairly and equitably managed from employee to employee. Instructional coaches are widely perceived as positive and enthusiastic employees, but they, too, understandably push back against evaluations that they view as unfair or inconsistent. Ensuring a clear focus on what the purpose of a particular evaluation is critical as a starting point to ensure not only that evaluation involves accountability for the organization but also fairness and helpfulness for the employee.

For instructional coaches, sound periodic evaluation has several benefits.

Sound evaluation

1.   ensures that the right people are in the right roles,

2.   helps leaders to identify (and, therefore, provide) appropriate training and resources for coaches,

3.   ensures alignment of what coaches do with the goals of the school or district by adhering to standards of best coaching practice,

4.   assists administrators in providing the most useful feedback to coaches on their performance by aligning with standards of best coaching practice, and

5.   assists coaches in highlighting successes and targeting the best goals for improvement.

✅ SOUND EVALUATION CHECKLIST

SOUND EVALUATION...	✅
Ensures that the right people are in the right roles	○
Helps leaders to identify appropriate training and resources for coaches	○
Ensures alignment of what coaches do with the goals of the school or district	○
Assists administrators in providing the most useful feedback to coaches on their performance	○
Assists coaches in highlighting successes and targeting the best goals for improvement	○

For instructional coaching programs, sound periodic evaluation can support the improvement of the organization as a whole (whether school- or district-based). Evaluating coaching programs fosters

1. the use of research-based standards in determining whether coaching is having the intended effect (Clardy, 1997),

2. accountability by examining the outcomes of what the coaches are doing (Clardy, 1997),

3. the best decisions regarding the use of funds for training and resources (Clardy, 1997), including professional development for new and veteran coaches,

4. accountability not only for coaches but also for school and district leadership in supporting coaching success,

5. alignment of the coaching program with the organization's mission and goals (Clardy, 1997), and

6. advocacy for the continued funding and support for coaching programs because of the evaluation's focus on data and evidence.

REASONS TO EVALUATE COACHING PROGRAMS CHECKLIST

EVALUATING COACHING PROGRAMS FOSTERS	✅
the use of research-based standards (Clardy, 1997)	○
accountability by examining outcomes (Clardy, 1997),	○
the best decisions regarding the use of funds for training and resources (Clardy, 1997),	○
accountability not only for coaches but also for school and district leadership in supporting coaching success,	○
alignment of the coaching program with the organization's mission and goals (Clardy, 1997), and	○
advocacy for the continued funding and support for coaching programs	○

AN EVALUATION COMPLICATION FOR INSTRUCTIONAL COACHES

One added complication particular to coaching is the historical role of instructional coaches in teacher evaluation processes. Often, leaders require teachers who are on performance improvement plans to work with coaches. This requirement can be a minefield for coaches in several ways, but the biggest concern is that it places the coach in the role of a quasi-evaluator and supervisor. Most coaches are peers of teachers and thus should not be placed (overtly or covertly) in a supervisory role.

The National Labor Relations Act (as cited in Fleischer, 2018) defines a supervisor as an "individual having authority ... to hire, transfer, suspend, lay off, recall, promote, discharge, assign, reward, or discipline other employees, or responsibility to direct them, or to adjust their grievances, or effectively to recommend such action" (p. 422). In a school, this definition applies to the members of the administrative team, not the instructional coach. Yet, because administrators often perceive coaches as "less threatening" to a teacher than administrators or because having the coach manage the teacher feels faster and easier for the administrators, they ask coaches to take on some aspects of that role.

In their coaching roles in schools, Sharon and Michelle were often put into such situations. In Sharon's case, more than once, school or district administrators would call her into the office and explain the issues they were having with a teacher's performance and the teacher's uncertain job status (communicating all of this to the coach—the employee's peer—is another human resources no-no). When telling her that the employee's improvement was now Sharon's "project," the administrator nearly always said something like, "This will all be so much better coming from you."

No, it wasn't. Having a supervisor place you on an improvement plan is bad enough, but then having a peer (not the boss) communicate your job status and the improvement plan to you is doubly embarrassing, as well as inappropriate. The teachers that Sharon worked with in those situations were humiliated, and they showed the defensiveness and resistance that come with feeling humiliated.

Meanwhile, on the other side of the country, Michelle had nearly identical experiences with compulsory coaching. Not until she and her fellow instructional coaches had been working with Jim for years did she have the language and understanding to engage in difficult conversations with leaders to argue that the practice should stop.

For the reasons just mentioned, never once did that forced "coaching" with Michelle or Sharon result in long-term positive change. The teachers kept their jobs, but once they were off their improvement plan, they went back to the way they had taught before, and they were embarrassed and sometimes defensive in front of Michelle and Sharon for the duration of their time in the same school building. Working with the coach was, for them, a sign of failure.

Not only does this quasi-supervisory role make a research-based partnership approach to coaching (as described in chapter 2) more challenging for the coach, it also blurs the line between coaching and evaluation. Evaluation conversations can be a launching point for coaching (offering the teacher the option of coaching support is a great idea), but evaluation and supervision are not the coach's job; they are the supervisor's job.

THE IMPORTANCE OF CLARITY

Without exception, lack of role clarity is the biggest barrier we see to instructional coaching having the greatest impact on students. Jim (Knight, 2017, 2022) has written increasingly on this topic because it is a pervasive, unintended consequence of failure to use research to develop a coaching program. The most common scenario we see in terms of how coaching positions become part of a school district is this:

STEP 1: Leaders see that teachers need support (with new standards, new programs, a growing concern about students, etc.).

STEP 2: "Instructional coaches" are hired but usually without a specific job description or a clear understanding of the research on instructional coaching that moves student data.

STEP 3: The coach begins working to support teachers but without knowing which coaching tasks most directly benefit students or how to prioritize the tasks. The coach's leaders indicate that they're not sure about that either, but remain confident that they'll work it out.

STEP 4: Soon, the coach (perceived as the rare adult in the building with "time on her hands") becomes overwhelmed with the growing number of "other duties as assigned" that she ends up having little or no time to implement the kind of coaching that research shows can move students academically, behaviorally, or in terms of their engagement (Knight, 2017).

The assumption when creating coaching programs is this: "If we hire people to support teachers, and teachers feel more supported, then students will grow." Unfortunately, the research indicates that assumption is false. The truth is that coaching "support" must involve particular elements and processes in order to result in a positive student impact. When coaches approach teachers as partners to work on student-focused goals that the teacher has set (with the coach's support), and the coach provides support until students hit that goal, then student data move (Knight, 2017).

All of the other tasks that coaches do (coordinating standardized testing, analyzing school data, coordinating professional learning communities, substitute teaching, etc.) may make teachers feel supported, but they do not have a strong research-documented student impact. Because coaches are often assigned to work on those other tasks instead of student-focused classroom goals, schools and districts won't see growth in students and will come to believe that coaching doesn't work. The problem is not that coaching doesn't work. Coaching works. The problem is the prevalent confusion about *which tasks* coaches need to do in order for coaching to work for students.

Coaching is essential for deep learning and change. Sustainable learning only happens in real life, or what Jim calls "learning in action."

Goals make learning real. When teachers have a goal that really matters to them, they want to learn and apply new ideas. They want real learning. The goal is only emotionally compelling for them if it is based on reality and they get to choose it. This is a lot to ask from a professional learning experience, but with the support of a coach, the teacher has a guide throughout the process. For teachers to experience real learning in action, coaches need the time and ability to create the right learning environments for teachers. Coaches cannot do that when their time is stretched in so many other directions.

Not surprisingly, the clarity issue is also at the heart of the confusion surrounding evaluation of coaches and coaching programs. Clarity permeates every aspect of evaluation:

» Districts can't create the right coach evaluation form and measure the right things if they're not sure what the coach does (or should be doing).
» Districts can't place the right people in the right roles if they're not clear on what those roles should look like.
» Districts can't support coaches with training and resources if they don't understand the coaching research and the coaching role.
» Feedback from supervisors won't mean much if administrators and coaches lack understanding about the coaching role.
» A lack of clarity about coaching makes fair, valid, and replicable evaluation of coaching programs nearly impossible because the people involved are all defining that role and its intent differently.

Leaders and coaches can improve role clarity in several ways that we will describe in this book:

» Clear evaluation rubrics and forms
» Clear and helpful evaluation conversations

- » Clear job descriptions and hiring procedures
- » Ongoing communication based on evaluations of both coaches and programs

The focus on clarity is one we will revisit time and again because it's one that schools and districts need to revisit to ensure sound hiring practices, evaluation practices, and school program decisions.

Where We Need to Be

EXPECTATIONS AND PROCESSES

One of our primary goals for this book is to provide schools and school districts with a guide and resources for evaluating coaches and coaching programs. We believe that, with clarity about the coaching role and the creation of the environment necessary to make that role a reality, coaches and coaching programs can achieve excellence in the form of improved student learning and engagement.

Evaluation processes should not merely follow laws surrounding employee evaluation; they should also include an aspirational element for employees. Human resources laws and policies sometimes have their basis in "bad actors"—employers who treated their employees unfairly and thus necessitated new policy to remedy that poor and/or discriminatory behavior. Thus, those laws and policies are often a reaction to poor leadership and sometimes provide only a minimum standard for both employers and employees. According to Amy Edmondson in *The Fearless Organization* (2019), employees do not perform best when leaders hold them to minimum standards. Just like students in positive classroom environments, employees perform best when leaders hold them to high standards and also provide a psychologically safe environment that encourages risk-taking and does not punish failure when trying something new.

Research-based standards of performance change an evaluation conversation from "What do I need to do to keep my coaching job?" to "What can I do to be a [more] excellent coach?"

In this book, we provide standards for accomplished coaching practice and coaching programs. Those standards support role clarity not only for coaches but also for their supervisors because administrator support is so central to coaching success. Most coaching evaluation processes today don't explicitly align with what the research says coaches should do to support teachers and students, so we provide specific guidelines for building that into coaching evaluation systems. Without research-based standards, evaluation is counterproductive because it's not measuring the kind of coaching that makes a difference for kids. (See chapters 2 and 3 for more information.) And because these standards are standards of excellence, they also provide that aspirational component by explicitly outlining what accomplished coaches do.

Building an evaluation program based on standards for what coaches should do benefits not only students and teachers but also schools and school districts. According to Alan Clardy, in *Studying Your Workforce* (1997), for organizations to make any kind of change that positively affects an organization and demonstrates its intended outcome (in this case, a change in coaching evaluation), organizations need to ensure the presence and alignment of three things:

1. **ACCOUNTABILITY** (What does research say employees should do [standards of performance] to achieve the intended outcome of this change? Are our employees doing that?);

2. **TRAINING** (Are we providing research-based training that aligns with what we want employees to do to make the change happen? What do our results indicate they need in future training to make the change?); and

3. **STRATEGIC ALIGNMENT** (Does this change support the long-term mission and objectives of the organization? How do we know?).

When such an aligned change is implemented, Clardy (1997) asserts, the organization will see interconnected benefits:

» The organization sees measurable gains [for teachers and students], *which leads to*
» better identification of problems [for teachers and students] based on those data, *which leads to*
» better identification of training needs [for employees], *which leads to*
» more learning on the part of employees [teachers and then students], *which leads to*
» better employee [teachers and then student] performance, *which leads to*
» better allocation of resources toward the organization's mission and objectives overall.

Moving an evaluation system to that level of positive change is not easy, but it is achievable. That process starts with clarity and standards.

A PROCESS FOR IMPROVEMENT

"Getting better" has always been a core theme of our work. In fact, coaching itself is fundamentally a conversation about getting better. Evaluation, too, should be a way of getting better, especially for coaches. If we want schools to move away from functioning as cultures of reward and punishment to functioning as cultures of growth and improvement, a focus on coaching is critical. Instructional coaches continually ask teachers questions like,

» "What do students need to do differently?"
» "What would that change look like?"
» "How would you measure that change?"
» "What do you want to try to bring about that change?"

Coaches are the key improvement specialists in the building. Naturally, their evaluation needs to function as an improvement process as well so that they are always improving, too. When coaches and coaching programs have an aspirational set of standards to work toward, and when they receive the support they need to meet those standards, the district can expect improvement in the coach, in the coaching program, and for the entire school or district.

If coaches continue to be evaluated based on the process for a different job (the teacher evaluation form, the guidance counselor form, etc.), the coaching role is diminished, coaches may sense that they are unimportant to the school or district, and they may end up feeling *misunderstood, mistreated,* and *overwhelmed*—three adjectives that usually result in an employee leaving his position. To keep coaches feeling supported and purposeful in their coaching roles, providing them with an evaluation that is both accurate and aspirational is key.

How We Get to Where We Need to Be

Along with *clarity*, the terms that appear nearly as a mantra throughout this book are *research, standards,* and *data*. Those three words are no strangers to educators, and can feel like harbingers of dry reading to come, but they're not. They are the critical elements of a vibrant evaluation system that helps coaches to feel valued and builds coaching programs that are strong and that significantly influence instruction and school culture.

RESEARCH

We can't know what coaches should be doing to positively affect student outcomes without a strong understanding of coaching that works. Jim's research of the past 20+ years is our guide in this area. In chapters 2 and 3, we'll describe that research via the Seven Success Factors for effective instructional coaching programs (Knight, 2022), which shape our coaching standards. We'll particularly describe the Impact Cycle, the research-based coaching process that not only improves teaching in classrooms but also provides data to tie coaching directly to student growth. The specific tasks of the coaching cycle are often a missing piece of current coach evaluations, so using the Impact Cycle as a framework can be an important step in gaining clarity for both administrators and coaches.

STANDARDS

The old adage of "What gets measured gets done" is true in coaching, too. We can't measure what we want to happen in coaching if we're not clear on what coaching is. The standards we'll describe in chapters 2 and 3 are the ones that guide our ICG Coaching Certification process (for resources on that process, visit https://instructionalcoaching.com/certifications/).

If coaches and coaching programs are expected to have a demonstrable impact on student data, understanding those standards is key. Because coaching positions and programs are often created without a focus on research or a specific coaching philosophy, coaches and leaders sometimes express surprise when learning the elements of coaching that are important in student success. Peeling back the layers of perception to get clarity about what actually works best is the job of standards, and that clarity aids everyone in moving coaching forward.

DATA

Districts can't ensure the fairness, validity, and replicability of an evaluation system without using measurable and reliable data to determine how well employees and programs are meeting the standards. One of the most important areas of learning for us in developing the ICG Coaching Certification process was determining which kinds of data and evidence in coaching are most helpful, including which ones may work for evaluation but not certification and vice versa. chapters 2 and 3 explain the data we find to be most helpful for evaluation, including feedback from piloting our evaluation tools and audit process with educators in school districts.

᎒᎒᎒

Certainly, schools and school districts need evaluation for its most basic purposes: promotion, correction, discipline, and termination. But we want more. In most ways, evaluation of adult employees will never mirror the evaluation of student academic progress. After all, we can hire adults who already have certain skills and knowledge, but students come to school for the very development of those things. But one element of crossover between evaluating children and evaluating adults can be a focus on learning and improvement.

As a middle school writing teacher, Michelle used rubrics to evaluate her students' work. But those rubrics weren't in place just to give students a grade and a summative judgment about the quality of their work; they also served as a teaching tool. Rubrics enabled Michelle to give students regular feedback to improve their writing. They spurred conversations about students' development as writers overall. They recognized not only areas that needed improvement but also areas that were strong. We hope that our focus on research, standards, and data for coaching evaluation will function in the same way—as a prompt for dialogue, as a recognition of areas for growth, and as a way for coaches to feel seen, acknowledged, celebrated, and understood.

Coaches like Malikah (like teachers and students nationwide) are extraordinarily patient with inadequate evaluation systems. They will work hard every day regardless of what that system looks like. But they deserve more. At the very least, they deserve their own evaluation form. Beyond that, they deserve an evaluation system that understands what coaches do to bring about growth for students, a system that treats their job as its own profession, and a system that fosters in them a desire to improve and the feeling that they are supported in taking risks to improve. Like students and teachers, coaches deserve the best.

OUR HOPE FOR THIS BOOK

————

We wrote this book to address the lack of a

comprehensive evaluation process for instruc-

tional coaches and coaching programs because

of its serious consequences for schools—and ulti-

mately, students. Coaching is a key leverage point

for improvement in schools. Coaches play a critical

role in school improvement because, if learning is

going to improve for kids, and improvement is going

to happen through better instruction, then we need

instructional coaches, and we need coaches doing

what research shows brings about the deepest

changes for students.

To guide you in using this book, the chapters are laid out in a consistent way.

 Each chapter begins with a **LEARNING MAP** depicting the key concepts in the chapter. We are visual people, and we hope this is helpful to you.

Each chapter ends with four reflective sections:

TO SUM UP provides a summary of each chapter.

MAKING IT REAL describes practical actions that educators can take to turn the ideas in each chapter into actions.

REFLECTION QUESTIONS are intended to prompt readers to make connections and examine ideas about each chapter's content.

GOING DEEPER introduces resources (mainly books) that readers can explore to extend their knowledge of the ideas and strategies in each chapter.

Throughout the book, you will also find the resources such as evaluation forms and resources to help guide you in making your evaluation processes as helpful as possible.

To Sum Up

» Most school districts do not have an evaluation process that is aligned well with the coaches' job and that provides good data on the success of the overall coaching program.

» Sound coaching evaluation begins with research-based standards of accomplished coaching practice.

» The evaluation process should not be used only to gather data for job retention, disciplinary action, or dismissal; it should be an improvement process that celebrates the good work that coaches are doing and helps coaches work toward excellence.

» Research on instructional coaching that moves student data must be the guide for developing standards, evaluation rubrics, and conversations about evaluation data.

Making It Real

To make improved evaluation real, we recommend two activities that will establish where your evaluation process is and what may need to change.

1.   First, examine the good and bad experiences you've had with employee evaluations (either as the evaluator or the employee). For the positive ones, what structures were in place that made the experience a good one? For the negative ones, what could have been done more constructively that would have improved the situation?

2.   To get started in creating a new process that maximizes the good experiences and minimizes the bad, reflect on the elements of your school or district's current process for evaluating instructional coaching and coaching programs. Cull all of the evaluation forms and guidelines that your school or district is using for coaches to see the tasks the current process encourages and those it does not. Is the role of coaches clearly defined and communicated throughout the district and reflected in the evaluation tools? Use the Reflection Questions below to prompt you in this area, and also consider seeking input from others who are involved in the evaluation process. Clarity moving forward begins with clarity about where you are now.

⟳ Reflection Questions

What was most valuable in this chapter?

What do you like about the way coaches or coaching programs are currently evaluated?

What are your current frustrations with how coaches or coaching programs are evaluated?

Does your coaching program have a guiding philosophy or set of research grounding it? Are coaching roles evaluated according to that research?

....

....

....

Are any aspects of coaching evaluation unclear to you?

....

....

....

....

....

....

What kinds of data do you use in the evaluation process for
coaches or coaching programs?

....

....

....

....

....

....

Going Deeper

One element of evaluation that is important to explore is the necessity of working to overcome people's negative mindset about the concept of evaluation, let alone the reality of it. For some, talking about evaluation is almost like talking about a traumatic experience. Communicating clearly about the purposes and goals of evaluation with employees is a good start, but that alone won't compensate for a history of perceived unfair and, in some cases, humiliating evaluation situations. Working to make evaluation clearer, fairer, and more helpful doesn't erase years of feeling misunderstood or even maligned by previous evaluators. Evaluators need to work diligently to communicate not only the fairness of the process but also the evaluator's genuine focus on improvement and on the best interests of the employees to change those past perceptions. Resources such as Jim Knight (2016), Shane Lopez (2013), C. R. Snyder (2003), Edgar Schein (2009), and Douglas Stone and Sheila Heen (2014) can provide leaders with the resources to navigate the affective as well as the cognitive domains of evaluation practices.

CHAPTER 2

EVALUATING INSTRUCTIONAL COACHES

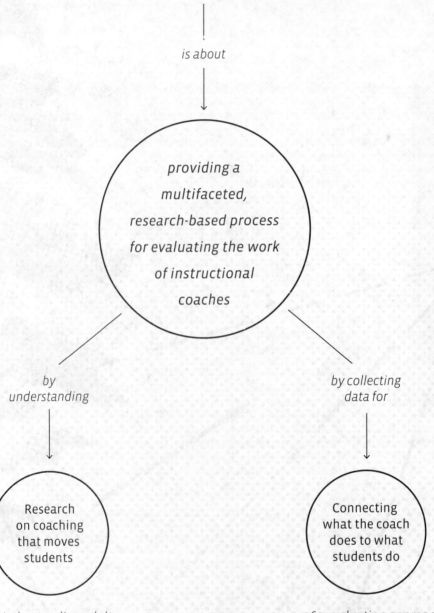

is about

providing a
multifaceted,
research-based process
for evaluating the work
of instructional
coaches

*by
understanding*

*by collecting
data for*

Research
on coaching
that moves
students

Connecting
what the coach
does to what
students do

- Understanding adults
  and change as the
  foundation
- The Seven Success
  Factors as the frame

- 360-evaluation approach
- Coach evaluation tools
- Evidence for evaluation
- Better feedback and
  evaluation conversations

CHAPTER

02

EVALUATING
INSTRUCTIONAL COACHES

 SNAPSHOT:

This chapter presents suggestions for how to create

a process for evaluating instructional coaches. It

delves into specific aspects of employee evaluation

and how to align evaluation with the research on

instructional coaching. You can skip this chapter

and move to chapter 3 if you are focused more on

evaluating instructional coaching programs and

not on evaluating individual coaches as employees.

Jacob served in several unofficial teacher-leader capacities in teacher support and as a professional developer in his middle school for years before becoming an official instructional coach.

Because the coaching role was newly established in Jacob's school, no evaluation form existed that captured all the elements of his role. He did have a job description, but it focused mostly on implementation support of various school district programs, not on the coaching role itself. Nonetheless, his conversations with his principal and district leaders clearly indicated that he was expected to provide implementation support, to coach teachers on their goals for their students, and to coordinate professional learning in his building. Jacob enjoyed all three roles and wanted to do them well, but without an evaluation form that described those jobs specifically and without a rubric for excellent performance, he had no gauge for what "well" was, let alone "excellence."

Because his role was new, Jacob, like Malikah in chapter 1, felt assured that his leaders would "work it out" and settle on an evaluation process that would help him to know how he was doing and what he should do to improve. In the years that he served in that role, they tried using the teacher evaluation form (not helpful), they tried using the district-based instructional coach evaluation form (a little more helpful but still not aligned with his actual job), and finally they tried a general portfolio-based process that Jacob suggested. The portfolio process helped him to communicate more fully what he was actually doing at school than the previous forms did, but it still involved no clear rubric for excellent coach performance.

Jacob's leaders went out of their way to be flexible and to ensure that he was never unfairly "scored down" on his annual evaluation because of issues with the process. Still, the situation left his leaders frustrated, and it left Jacob feeling like no one really knew how he spent his days. Worse, he had no real sense of whether he was making a difference for students as a coach. As a teacher, he had evidence of what was working and not working for his students each day, which helped him to try to do better the next day, so not knowing whether his coaching had an impact on students was truly agonizing.

When he relocated and began working as a coach in a different state, Jacob discovered that the issues he had experienced with coaching evaluation were not unique to his previous coaching position. In fact, they were common concerns among coaches and school leaders. Jacob wondered, "Will there come a time when I introduce myself as an 'instructional coach' and I won't have to explain what that means?" and "Will anyone ever figure out how to evaluate my performance?"

ASSESSMENT VERSUS EVALUATION

The terms *assessment* and *evaluation* are often used interchangeably, which can create confusion. For clarity, we use *assessments* to refer to individual tools that provide data on an aspect of performance or programs. We use the term *evaluation* to refer to the examination of all assessments of an employee's performance or of a program to determine future performance or program goals. Our assessment tools may be used as part of ongoing formative assessment to make small adjustments during the school year as well as to inform the annual evaluation of the coach or the overall coaching program.

Jacob's story highlights the connection between the problems we see in coaching evaluation (as described in chapter 1) and what we see as possibly the greatest barrier to instructional coaching being able to truly maximize its potential for the benefit of students: the lack of role clarity. The word *coaching* itself leads to some of the problems around role clarity, especially for people who work in schools. For some educators, the term immediately conjures up the image of a coach in an athletic setting. For others, the word reminds them of the mentor they were assigned when they first started teaching, that safe person to whom they could run on those really tough early days. For still others, a coach is someone who assists people on performance improvement plans to keep their jobs, someone who "fixes" people and problems.

Due to these different perceptions of the term *instructional coach*, the role is defined differently not only from district to district and school to school but also from coach to coach and teacher to teacher. Even when the school and the coach work hard to convey to faculty members what an "instructional coach" is, those previous perceptions of the term often persist, making the coach's work difficult and possibly affecting the evaluation process.

This chapter provides schools and school districts with research, processes, and tools that aid in gaining role clarity so as to better evaluate instructional coaches. For too long, administrators and coaches have made up evaluation as they go. But "making it up as they go" does not support coaches in improving, and it can make sustaining coaching positions difficult as well. Often, school boards request justification for coaching roles, and a lack of clarity around the coaches' role and how to evaluate its success feeds misperceptions about coaching that too frequently result in elim-inating coaching positions. Good evaluation practices are impera-tive to sustain research-based classroom support for teachers.

We begin this chapter by examining what research-based instructional coaching looks like and then describe the data collection necessary to find evidence of that research in actual coaching practice. Additionally, we propose the key elements of a "360" coach evaluation process, introduce tools we've created to inform that process, and describe how to ensure effective and humanizing evaluation conversations.

Research on Coaching That Moves Students

UNDERSTANDING ADULTS AND CHANGE AS THE FOUNDATION

A common misperception about instructional coaches is that their most important attribute is a deep knowledge of instruction and instructional strategies. Certainly, understanding best instructional practices is an important element of coaching, but it's not the most important one, according to our research (Knight, 2007, 2011, 2017; Knight et al., 2010). The most important quality of an instructional coach is an understanding of how adults learn and change and how to approach adults about change.

In our workshops on coaching, we share some of the most compelling research in the area of adults and change (Davenport, 2005; Lopez, 2013; Pink, 2009; Prochaska, 1994; Schein, 2009; Stone & Heen, 2014), but changing our beliefs about how adults learn and grow can be difficult, especially for educators. Given that the vast majority of people who are in teacher support roles in school districts were once teachers themselves, perhaps this shouldn't come as a surprise. During their time in the classroom, they were the "adult in charge," and their charges were children. To maintain a productive and orderly learning environment, many teachers assume an authoritative posture, and that teacher-student dynamic mirrors a parent-child dynamic. Students overwhelmingly cooperate with that dynamic because they usually accept the stance of "I'm the child, and you're the adult, so I have to do what you say."

When teachers with that mindset move into a teacher support role such as coaching, that authoritative posture often comes with them, and they (either consciously or subconsciously) view themselves as the "teacher" and the teachers they support as the "students." But the trouble is, as Thomas Davenport (2005) and Edgar Schein (2009) point out, adults don't respond well to that dynamic. They are professionals. They do not want to be treated like children. They want support, not a teacher. They want a partner, not a parent.

Because of their resistance to that teacher-student dynamic, adults often resist the support they are offered (whether coaching, professional development activities, new programs, etc.), and the coach (who has acted only with good intent) can't understand why. The coach's lack of knowledge of instruction and instructional strategies is not what causes the resistance; the way the coach approaches teachers in supporting them is what causes the resistance.

For these reasons, understanding adults and change needs to play an important role in evaluating coaches' performance. Therefore, our coaching model is grounded in partnership not because partnership is humanizing and respectful (though it is those things, too), but because partnership lowers teacher resistance and engages them more deeply in coaching. *How* the coach interacts with teachers is as important as *what* the coach and teacher are working on. This can be frustrating for leaders who want coaches to "fix" teachers and classrooms—and to do so quickly. The "fixer" approach doesn't work. Partnership does.

In a study involving coaches across the state of Florida (Knight et al., 2010), researchers identified the attributes of exceptional coaches from the perspectives of a wide range of stakeholders—coaches, teachers, principals, and district or regional coaching coordinators. That research found four themes across respondents that describe effective coaches:

» **THEME 1:** Effective coaches embody an **array of interpersonal strengths** that enables them to develop a collaborative and professional working relationship with teachers.

» **THEME 2:** Effective coaches are **effective communicators**, which includes providing direct, nonevaluative feedback while listening to the perspectives, opinions, and concerns of teachers.

» **THEME 3:** Effective coaches possess a wide range of knowledge and skills and are resourceful, yet they **continue to seek out and acquire new knowledge** to benefit teachers.

» **THEME 4:** Effective coaches **creatively generate coaching opportunities and relish the chance to work with teachers** while fostering a cohesive school community.

Each of these themes directly involves the way the coach approaches teachers as partners in the coaching relationship. The common perception that "the best teachers make the best coaches" isn't necessarily true. While knowledge of instructional strategies is important (we describe that more fully when examining Factor Four: The Instructional Playbook in this chapter), it is the coach's approach that can make or break the teacher's willingness to be coached in the first place. As one coaching coordinator in the study explained, "The best teacher in the world is not always going to be the best coach because the best teacher doesn't always feel comfortable working with adults." Understanding adults and change provides the foundation for coaching, and thus for evaluating coaches.

With partnership as our foundation, based on an understanding of adults and change, we next explore our Seven Success Factors for effective instructional coaching programs, which are also central to sound coach evaluation.

FACTOR ONE:

THE PARTNERSHIP PRINCIPLES

Jim's doctoral work resulted in his first book, *Instructional Coaching: A Partnership Approach to Improving Instruction* (Knight, 2007), in which he introduced the Partnership Principles. Coaches can use the Partnership Principles to set goals for ways in which they can be more partnership-like in their interactions with their colleagues.

» **EQUALITY:** Coaches value teachers and their abilities as much as they value their own. Everyone on the team may have different skills and areas for growth, but everyone on the team is valued. Each person matters equally regardless of their role or position on the career ladder.

» **CHOICE:** To treat teachers as professionals means empowering them with professional discretion. If teachers only act in response to mandates with no choice or autonomy about how they do their job, then they are not being treated as professionals. Choice is crucial for their engagement in change.

» **VOICE:** Effective coaches want to hear what others have to say, and they are willing to encourage others to use the voices in conversations and to make decisions.

» **REFLECTION:** In encouraging teachers to look back at where a student concern began, to look at the status of that issue now, and to look ahead to what they want that situation to look like moving forward, coaches encourage teachers to use their voice and at the same time they gain important information that helps them to offer better ideas to teachers (Knight, 2016).

» **DIALOGUE:** In a dialogue, teachers and coaches feel safe in voicing their ideas for coming up with the best solutions for moving forward. Teachers do not feel as if they must do what the coach says but are open to the coach's ideas, just as the coach is open to the teacher's ideas.

» **PRAXIS:** Both children and adults learn most deeply when given the chance to apply what they're learning to real-life situations, even to experiment with it. Coaches working in partnership with teachers encourage an inquiry-based approach to adult learning, not a control-based approach.

» **RECIPROCITY:** Because partners are open to new ideas and neither assumes they have all the answers, both coach and teacher learn a great deal by working with each other.

FACTOR TWO:
THE IMPACT CYCLE

The Impact Cycle process (see Figure 2.1) developed out of years of coaching research (Knight, 2017). The three stages of the cycle can appear deceptively simple; however, to be performed well, they involve a sensitivity to the complexities of human interactions to support teachers staying engaged and hopeful about improving outcomes for students.

Figure 2.1:

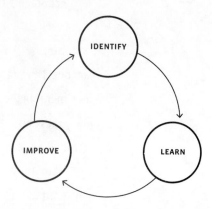

The Impact Cycle involves three phases: Identify, Learn, and Improve (Knight, 2017). Throughout all three phases, the coach works to maintain a partnership relationship with the teacher that focuses on respect, collaboration, and reflection, not on control.

IDENTIFY: In the Identify phase, the coach assists the teacher in doing three things:

» Getting a clear picture of classroom reality (What's really going on with the students in the area about which the teacher is concerned?)

» Setting a goal for student improvement in that area (what we call a PEERS goal: a Powerful, Emotionally Compelling, Easy, Reachable, Student-Focused goal)

» Choosing an instructional strategy to help the students hit the goal

LEARN: During the Learn phase, the coach helps the teacher to implement the instructional strategy that the teacher chose in the Identify phase by

» Clearly describing the strategy with the help of a one-page description and a checklist [see Factor Four: Instructional Playbook])

» Providing modeling of the strategy at the teacher's discretion

» Encouraging time for the teacher to practice the strategy

IMPROVE: The final phase, the Improve phase, involves the teacher implementing the strategy. The coach supports the teacher in whatever ways the teacher requests (including data collection, data analysis, troubleshooting concerns, etc.) to make any neces-sary adaptations until the goal is met. Topics of conversations that may occur during the Improve phase include

- » Confirming direction
- » Reviewing progress
- » Inventing improvements
- » Planning next actions

The Impact Cycle process ensures a focus on student growth, not on perceived teacher deficits. Its emphasis on student-focused goals means it is a process that can provide data to directly tie the work of the coach with the teacher to student progress.

FACTOR THREE:
DATA

Effective instructional coaches are skilled in gathering data to help teachers set goals and to monitor progress on those goals. Michelle sees a clear difference between what her coaching looked like before her district began a concerted focus on goal setting with teachers as the focus of coaching and what coaching looked like afterwards.

Before goals became the focus, Michelle would approach a teacher in the hallway and ask, "How are things going?" And typically, the teacher would say, "Fine." When approaching another teacher, she would say, "How's using that new strategy going?" Again, she received a reply of "Fine." In approaching yet another teacher, she might try a different approach, asking, "Anything I can do to help you?," only to get the response, "No, thanks. I'm good." Despite Michelle's attempts to engage with teachers, not much deep conversation about classroom improvement happened because the conversations lacked focus.

Referring to specific goals changed the conversation. When Michelle asked, "What's the progress on your engagement goal?," she and the teacher had a deeper, more specific, and more helpful conversation. And when she asked a teacher a question like, "Does measuring your goal with that new tool work? How can I help?," again, the conversation became about what students were doing and how the classroom was changing. Goals make for deeper coaching, which makes for deeper change for students.

Similarly, midway through a five-year research project in which Ann coached teachers, she started using the Identify Questions to help teacher set goals as part of the Impact Cycle (Knight, 2017) instead of her previous conversation starter, "How's it going?" Once that new structure started focusing the teachers on specific student-focused goals, they told Ann that they were much more reflective before each of their coaching sessions. As a result, the coaching sessions became more efficient and productive. In fact, teachers sometimes began answering the Identify Questions (in other words, they started setting goals) as soon as Ann set foot in their classroom.

Because goals are so important in coaching, data are crucial. A coach needs to have knowledge about various ways to measure changes in student academic achievement, student behavior, and student engagement, and they can assist and encourage teachers with frequent, clear, and helpful data collection on goals. Skill not only in collecting and analyzing data but also in using a partnership approach when discussing data is a marker of an accomplished coach.

FACTOR FOUR:
INSTRUCTIONAL PLAYBOOK

Once the teacher sets a goal, coaches need a collection of *High-Impact Instructional* strategies that they have at the ready when helping teachers to achieve goals for students, what we call an instructional playbook (Knight et al., 2020). Goal-setting conversations can be frustrating for teachers because they seek out coaching support in areas where they are genuinely concerned about their students' progress, so having a set of strategies that the coach has already vetted can alleviate both teacher and coach anxiety around choosing a strategy to hit that goal. Our book *The Instructional Playbook: The Missing Link for Translating Research Into Practice* (Knight et al., 2020) describes the process for creating a playbook in detail.

An instructional playbook consists of three key components:

1.   a one-page table of contents that lists *High-Impact Instructional* strategies in the areas where teachers are asking coaches for the most support,

2.   a one-page description of each of the strategies in the table of contents, and

3.   sufficient checklists for each one-page description so that the coach has an aid to clearly explain the strategy to the teacher and teachers have an aid to assist them in implementing the strategy with students.

Providing teachers with choices of strategies instead of advice or directives is central to the idea of partnership, and the playbook provides tangible evidence that the coach trusts the teacher's judgment and is flexible in approaching each classroom's needs. The playbook is a "living" document, one that coaches revise over time as student, teacher, and program needs change.

FACTOR FIVE:
COMMUNICATION HABITS AND SKILLS

Because the way that coaches approach teachers about coaching is key to coaching success, and because conversation is such a critical aspect of coach-teacher interactions, coaches need exceptionally strong communication habits and skills. Jim's book *Better Conversations: Coaching Ourselves and Each Other to Be More Credible, Caring, and Connected* (Knight, 2016) describes 10 communication habits that can help to set goals for improving how we interact with others both personally and professionally:

1. Demonstrate Empathy
2. Listen
3. Foster Dialogue
4. Ask Better Questions
5. Make Emotional Connections
6. Be a Witness to the Good
7. Find Common Ground
8. Control Toxic Emotions
9. Redirect Toxic Conversations
10. Build Trust

Constant attention to and development of these habits ensures a partnership approach with teachers and fosters a positive, collaborative, and more equitable school culture.

FACTOR SIX:
LEADERSHIP

Coaches are leaders in their schools, but because they are peers of the people they coach and not evaluators, their leadership looks different from that of school or district leaders. Coaches lead by building trusting relationships with teachers that result in teachers feeling safe to work with them in Impact Cycles. Such relationships allow teachers to be more honest and vulnerable with the coach, and that honesty and vulnerability are crucial in bringing about change that will affect students. Coaches demonstrate leadership through partnership, not through control. They encourage teachers to act as the decision-makers in their classrooms, and they trust teachers' intelligence and capabilities.

Coaches also lead by developing an exceptional level of instructional expertise that can aid teachers in setting and hitting their goals for students. Coaches share that knowledge as appropriate but do so dialogically as a partner and a peer, not as an "expert," "fixer," or evaluator.

These types of leadership qualities are challenging to develop not only because they differ from a more commanding and controlling view that many have of the term *leader*, but also because our impulse to want to help others can make us inadvertently treat them in ways that may feel to them like parenting, and thus control. Effective instructional coaches lead through their understanding of that dynamic and their continual self-awareness regarding how they're interacting with colleagues. Because their leadership engages teachers in deep change for students, coaches are powerful change agents who use their skills solely for the benefit of teachers and students.

FACTOR SEVEN:
SYSTEM SUPPORT

As mentioned in chapter 1, the need to improve coaching evaluation is one of the most common concerns related to coaching that we hear from districts—in particular, the need for school and district administrator support for coaching. Unless administrators, coaches, and teachers are all working from a shared understanding of what coaching is, coaches are not likely to get the support they need to have an impact on students.

A shared definition of instructional coaching helps to prevent two of the most common obstacles for coaches:

» role clarity and
» how coaches spend their time.

Our research-based definition of coaching aligns with the Identify, Learn, and Improve phases of the Impact Cycle (Knight, 2017):

Instructional coaches partner with teachers to

» Analyze current reality *(Identify phase)*
» Set goals *(Identify phase)*
» Identify *(Identify phase)* and explain *(Learn phase)* teaching strategies to hit the goals
» Provide support until goals are met *(Improve phase)*

This definition surprises coaches and leaders who are unfamiliar with coaching research because of its specificity and because it does not involve many of the tasks that many associate with coaching. In our Impact Cycle workshops, we discuss the issue of how schools or districts define instructional coaching and the impact that a lack of role clarity for coaches has on schools. In those sessions, we share a list of the most common activities we see coaches perform around the world.

» Providing and managing resources
» Walk-through observations
» Substitute teaching
» Cafeteria/bus duty
» Leading professional learning communities
» Conducting meetings
» Giving presentations
» Testing coordination
» Personal knowledge building

- » Mentoring
- » Pull-out interventions
- » Implementation support
- » Impact Cycle coaching with teachers

In fact, several coaches in those workshops say they are expected to do everything on this list (which is by no means comprehensive), that it is a fairly accurate job description for them. Because each task is time-consuming, coaches also say that they feel like they are doing few or none of their tasks well and have little guidance on which tasks are priorities.

Because coaches want to fulfill the expectations of everyone in the school, their work doesn't necessarily register a student impact because they are focused on so many activities that are helpful to adults but do not have a measurable impact on students. The last item on the list, Impact Cycle coaching, is the one item that has a measurable impact on students. Leaders who want coaches to work in Impact Cycles for student improvement need to help coaches establish role clarity and make sure coaches have time to do that work.

If coaches don't know which tasks they should focus on and how much time to allot to those tasks, time quickly becomes a barrier to Impact Cycle coaching. Strong system support involves role clarity, a clear set of priorities for the coach's time, regular meetings with the coach, and, most important, a shared belief in and understanding of coaching.

System support also means establishing a culture of coaching that is focused on growth instead of rewards and punishments. To foster a learning culture throughout a school or district, coaching should not just be for teachers. Leaders need coaches too, and supporting and modeling coaching at all levels shows a respect for all educators' professionalism and potential.

Connecting What the Coach Does to What Students Do

For teachers to feel safe in being honest and vulnerable with an instructional coach, they need to have hope that coaching will help them with their goals for their students. The research on hope (Lopez, 2013; Snyder, 2003) is a touchstone for us when describing the importance of goals in coaching. According to Lopez (2013), to have hope in a given situation, a person needs three things:

1.   A goal that serves as a clear picture for them of how they want the situation to improve

2.   Clear pathways that help them to envision how they can achieve that goal

3.   Agency (the power, the autonomy) to successfully navigate those pathways on their way to the goal

Without an evaluation system with specific criteria, hiring and retaining coaches with the support and follow-up they need is nearly impossible (see chapter 4). Coaches and administrators should meet often to discuss the impact that coaching is having on students, and they need clear criteria for what effective coaching is for those discussions to move students forward. In many school districts, clear job descriptions and evaluation processes are in place for every employee role except for instructional coaches.

Like any other professionals, instructional coaches need a clear set of standards so they feel supported in learning and improving. The lack of a clear job description and a clear evaluation process not only frustrates coaches by not providing an accurate assessment of what they're doing, it also fails to provide an improvement process that includes setting aspirational goals.

To provide that aspirational component and to help coaches to set goals, we offer a 360-evaluation approach to coaching evaluation that includes standards, a rubric, and tools to establish what excellent coaching looks like.

360-EVALUATION APPROACH

Because of the importance of human interactions in instructional coaching, we advocate for a 360-evaluation approach to coaching evaluation. According to the Society for Human Resources Management (SHRM), 360-evaluation processes "... involve evaluations not only by an employee's supervisor, but also by peers, direct reports, and in some cases, internal or outside customers or clients" (Fleischer, 2018, p. 42). Unlike traditional evaluations that involve only the voices of evaluator and employee, 360 evaluations acknowledge the importance of the employee's performance on other employees and on the success of the organization overall by incorporating feedback from stakeholders.

According to Christian van Nieuwerburgh (2017), a 360-evaluation approach is "a more robust and generally accepted way of collecting work-related feedback" than traditional evaluations (p. 66). Our 360-evaluation approach for instructional coaches gathers feedback on the coaches' performance from the coaches themselves, the teachers they have coached, as well as administrators. Feedback from teachers is particularly powerful for coaches because the reciprocal nature of that dynamic reinforces partnership in a deep and real way by valuing the teacher's perspective in the process.

van Nieuwerburgh (2017) sees another positive benefit of 360 evaluations for coaches. When receiving feedback from multiple perspectives, coaches can use the information to target ways to improve coaching relationships moving forward. "From a coaching perspective, the report provides a very good starting point for discussion. Differences between the coachee's self-assessment and the responses of others would be an area of particular interest" (p. 66).

But despite its many benefits, a 360 evaluation can become problematic if everyone involved in the coach's evaluation does not have clarity surrounding the expectations of their involvement. As SHRM says, "Employers need to plan 360-degree evaluation programs with particular care and understand and clearly communicate to employees the procedures and objectives" (Fleischer, 2018, p. 42). For example, concerns such as confidentiality, how perception influences rankings on the forms, and consistency in providing support to each evaluator in using the forms should be addressed directly and openly from the start of the evaluation process.

One particular complication of a 360-evaluation approach involves the fact that most instructional coaching positions are still designated as "teacher" positions at the HR level and thus are in the same "bargaining unit" as teachers during union contract negotiations. As Aretha Young, Certification Team Leader with Harford County (MD) Public Schools explained to us, using a 360-evaluation approach solely for coaches and not for teachers may require additional policy or negotiation with the union (A. Young, personal communication, April 29, 2021). Using that approach with a group of employees as large as teachers may be unrealistic for a school district, so singling coaches out in this way may engender resistance from both teachers and coaches.

Sue Robertson, Chief Human Resource Officer with Beaverton (OR) School District, agrees and suggests that providing guidance and a specific process to administrators could make everyone more comfortable with a 360 approach. For example, districts could encourage the coach "to use 360 data on a quarterly or semester basis to gather personal feedback and set goals. The coach, in turn, could share how the information was used to grow one's practice during performance conversations with the administrator or in a written reflection" (S. Roberston, personal communication, April 18, 2021).

As with all elements of evaluation, communicating with stakeholders early and engaging them as part of creating fair coach evaluation will ensure that everyone understands and supports the evaluation system that evolves.

To develop a process for creating a sound coach evaluation process, we recommend these steps:

1. Examine our coaching standards (Appendix 1) to determine the parameters of the instructional coach role.

2. Create a job description for the coach role that aligns with the standards and indicators you chose.

3. Examine the instructional coach rubric (Appendix 2) to determine success criteria and ranges of performance for the tasks listed on the job description.

4. Determine the types of data you will accept as evidence of performance on the rubric.

5. Examine and modify the coach, teacher, and administrator feedback forms (Appendices 3, 4, and 5) to align 360 feedback with the standards and job description. Determine also how to distribute and collect those forms while ensuring confidentiality and HR standards surrounding feedback.

6. Determine the coach evaluation process parameters (time points for observations/evaluations during the school year, time points for various data pieces, etc.)

7. Determine how the employer will approach feedback with coaches and how the employer will create an environment conducive to encouraging the coach's voice in those conversations.

8. Develop a plan for how to communicate the evaluation process to stakeholders, including gathering feedback to improve the process.

DEVELOPING A 360-EVALUATION PROCESS FOR COACHES CHECKLIST

EVALUATING INSTRUCTIONAL COACHES	✓
Examine our coaching standards (Appendix 1) to determine the parameters of the instructional coach role.	○
Create a jonb description for the coach role that aligns with the standards and indicators you chose.	○
Examine the instructional coach rubric (Appendix 2) to determine success criteria and ranges of performance for the tasks listed on the job description.	○
Determine the types of data you will accept as evidence of performance on the rubric.	○
Examine and modify the coach, teacher, and administrator feedback forms (Appendices 3, 4, and 5) to align 360 feedback with the standards and job description. Determine also how to distribute and collect those forms while ensuring confidentiality and HR standards surrounding feedback.	○
Determine the coach evaluation process parameters (time points for observations/evaluations during the school year, time points for various data pieces, etc.)	○
Determine how the employer will approach feedback with coaches and how the employer will create an environment conducive to encouraging the coach's voice in those conversations.	○
Develop a plan for how to communicate the evaluation process to stakeholders, including gathering feedback to improve the process.	○

To provide a framework for what teacher, coach, and administrator contributions could look like in a 360-evaluation model, we include sample forms that align with our coaching standards around the Seven Success Factors.

ELOPMENT OF THE TOOLS

/ears, coaches, administrators, and school districts asked
o create an instructional Coaching Certification process.
trated with existing school and district coaching evaluation
esses, they wanted Jim to provide a process aligned with the
act Cycle. In 2017, the Instructional Coaching Group (ICG) began
eloping a process that would serve that purpose. What we
1d out quickly, though, was that, as with the term *coach*, the
1 *certification* has different meanings for different people.

ie people view a certification process as a training model in
ch a professional completes a workshop or coursework to gain
wledge in a particular area. For others (including us), a profes-
1al certification process is *a demonstration of current, accom-
hed practice*. As with the National Board Certification process
teachers, candidates for ICG Coaching Certification are not
:iving training in how to be coaches; rather, they are already
ching according to the Impact Cycle model and are demon-
ting excellence in that regard.

.chieve ICG Coaching Certification, candidates submit data,
:o, and documentation to fulfill two portfolio entries. During
iocess that can last anywhere from one to three years (candi-
:es have some flexibility in submitting and retaking entries),
didates reflect and target aspects of their coaching practice
t they want to improve (see www.instructionalcoaching.com/
:ifications for the current process in full).

.e first starting to develop the certification process, we have
wurked with two superb (and wonderfully patient) candidate
cohorts who helped us pilot the first iteration of the process to
determine what certification should look like. Starting in 2021,

Dear Coach,

This book, "Evaluating Instructional Coaching", is a thank you gift from the University of North Carolina for participating in our baseline data collection survey during our February monthly all-coaches' meeting.

We also appreciate you taking the time to complete the survey. Please don't ever hesitate to reach out to any of us.

Jen, Karen, and Roni

new candidates for certification follow the revised iteration of that process. From the beginning, we provided a set of standards (based on the Seven Success Factors) that candidates can use as a guide in creating the materials they submit for certification (see **Appendix 1**). However, we learned from our pilot candidate cohorts that standards and some scoring guidelines are not enough to help coaches measure their progress and improvement. Both the candidates and the instructional coaches who served as certification scorers requested a more specific rubric for identifying where candidates are along a continuum of excellence.

Creating a rubric for instructional coaches is challenging and takes time and effort. Michelle Lis, Coordinator of Instructional Coaching for Fairfax County (VA) Public Schools (FCPS), has worked to continually refine and improve their district's coaching program. Key Elements, aligned to the teacher evaluation rubric and standards, have been modified to reflect the work of instructional coaches. The FCPS teacher evaluation encompasses these categories:

» Professional Knowledge
» Instructional Planning
» Instructional Delivery
» Assessment of and for Student Learning
» Learning Environment
» Professionalism
» Student Academic Progress

In an FCPS instructional coach's evaluation, each of those categories includes performance indicators directly tied to the coaching role and a four-point rubric that demonstrates performance characteristics for the Highly Effective, Effective, Developing or Needs Improvement, and Ineffective rating points. The rubric is one of the most specific and helpful ones we have seen in the field. Michelle hopes to continue to revise the rubric to ensure that a focus on equity and culturally responsive teaching is included.

A rubric with the level of detail and complexity of the FCPS rubric is rare. Our certification pilot helped us to understand the helpfulness of a rubric not only for certification canddiates but also for the instructional field in general to assist school districts in creating fair and useful evaluation processes.

With the latest changes to the certification program, we made two modifications for these purposes:

1.   We added quality indicators to the standards (Appendix 1).

2.   We added guidance in the form of a rubric (or "Scoring Look-Fors," as we call them on the certification website) to aid candidates in determining where they are in their coaching practice and to assist scorers in evaluating candidate submissions (see www.instructionalcoaching.com/certifications/scoring for the current look-fors).

To assist schools and school districts in evaluating instructional coaches as employees in schools, we have adapted the scoring look-fors into a rubric to more specifically describe what excellent coaching looks like in practice (**Appendix 2**). The rubric is organized according to the Seven Success Factors and is organized by the Standards and Quality Indicators (Appendix 1).

Each tool in our 360-evaluation process is aligned with the most important elements of the standards and the rubric. Using these tools as part of a coach's evaluation provides evaluators with good data for measuring performance and good data for the coach to use to set goals.

TEACHER FEEDBACK FORM

The voices of teachers are imperative in evaluating instructional coaches and coaching programs. As we found in the research on the power of a partnership coaching approach, having data about the coach's interactions with teachers is crucial to fully measure a coach's impact. The best data about how well the coach is operating as a partner with teachers come from teachers.

One frustration that some of the candidates in our pilot cohorts expressed was that parts of their portfolio entries involve feedback from teachers and administrators—that part of their score is determined by the actions and opinions of others and not solely on their own merit and materials. The use of feedback from peers as part of an employee evaluation may concern school and district administrators in relation to coaches as well. If the success of coaching did not so critically hinge on how coaches interact with teachers, gaining evidence solely from coaches about their coaching might work. But the success of coaching *does* hinge on those interactions, and evaluators (whether certification scorers or employers) need evidence from teachers about how the coach works with them.

Appendix 3 presents a teacher feedback form that school districts can use as part of employee evaluation to encourage teacher voice in coach evaluation. To ensure consistency, the questions are aligned with the Seven Success Factors. Asking each teacher who worked with the coach the same questions and giving them the same answer options is important for several reasons:

» Asking the same questions and providing the same answer options makes the data more valid and reliable (Clardy, 1997).

» Providing space for written narratives by teachers would potentially risk revelations of confidential information or irrelevant information that would not be appropriate in the evaluation of an employee.

» Employers can ensure that the feedback that teachers are providing is aligned with job expectations.

» Coaches will have a higher level of psychological safety with the feedback process knowing that specific questions and answer choices are indeed the feedback data that they will be examining.

» Teachers will have a higher level of psychological safety to be honest in providing feedback because the form does not contain identifiers or request statements or narratives that could identify them.

COACH SELF-EVALUATION FORM

The second element of the 360-evaluation approach for instructional coaches is a self-evaluation component for the coaches themselves. Coaches are not likely to use the evaluation as a tool for growth if they do not receive the opportunity to reflect on their practice and set new goals for themselves. As van Nieuwerburgh notes (2017), coaches can use the feedback they receive from both teachers and administrators as ground for reflection on their practice, on important differences in perception across the various pieces of feedback, and as data for goal setting goals toward improvement.

The coach self-evaluation form in **Appendix 4** aligns with the questions on the teacher feedback form but is worded from the perspective of the coach. Unlike what we recommend with the teacher feedback form, districts could add space for the coach to add deeper written reflection. Allowing coaches to voice their thinking around their answers to the form's questions and to discuss other job issues beyond the scope of questions on the form is absolutely appropriate to ensure that they feel fully heard on their job performance. The design of this tool is similar to teacher self-evaluation tools that many districts already have in place.

ADMINISTRATOR FEEDBACK FORM

A 360-evaluation approach for coaches also involves school and/or district administrator feedback. The modification we urge leaders to consider in this area is to ensure that research-based coaching practices are part of that feedback. Because so many coach evaluation forms are modified versions of teacher evaluation forms or non-classroom personnel forms, specific elements of coaching are often absent.

Like the teacher and coach forms, our administrator form (**Appendix 5**) aligns with the Seven Success Factors. As with the coach self-evaluation form, districts can modify the form to include space for a narrative regarding the administrator's responses to the questions on the form or other aspects of the coach's job performance. The coach's supervising administrator will undoubtedly want to share more information on performance than the form's questions ask. The key aspect of the administrator form is that it sets Impact Cycle coaching as the standard for coaching excellence and includes it directly as part of the evaluation. Doing so reinforces role clarity for the coach and for leaders and shows a focus on coaching tasks that will help to bring about important change for students.

As with all things in coaching, the more clarity everyone has around processes and expectations, the more likely it is that the process will result in its intended outcomes. For the evaluation to accomplish more than "checking boxes" and to be an improvement process for the coach, the process should include specific steps for using the feedback in shaping the coach's future goals. Otherwise, "substantial time will have been wasted collecting useless and unused data" (Fleischer, 2018, p. 42).

MODIFYING THE TOOLS

Schools and districts should modify the forms we provide in this book as necessary to provide clarity for their staff members and to align with their system language. In 2020, we piloted the forms as part of a coaching audit process (described in chapter 3) that we conducted with Katy (TX) ISD. The leaders in Katy broke down some of our questions into more discrete parts based on the level of experience that different coaches had with the Impact Cycle, and they also wanted more questions focusing on the issue of the coach as an advocate for instructional improvement in schools. Their modifications were helpful and consistent with their system needs while still reinforcing the Seven Success Factors as critical in coaching success.

We conducted additional research on these forms by asking some of our long-term coaching partners to use them as part of individual coach evaluations during the 2019-2020 school year and to provide us feedback on their use. Respondents cited several benefits to using these forms for coaching evaluation:

» The forms are clear, and many evaluators liked the consistency in the wording of the items across the teacher, coach, and administrator forms.
» The forms set Impact Cycle coaching as the standard of practice, as opposed to all the "other duties as assigned" that coaches engage in but that do not significantly impact student growth.
» The inclusion of the reflection form for the coach ensures that the coach has a voice in the process.

Districts also noted some concerns or complications with using the forms.

» Some administrators may not have enough experience with the Impact Cycle to complete the forms.

» Some administrators may need convincing to consider artifacts, portfolios, and other evidence of coaching success instead of merely checking off items on a form.

As with any evaluation or data-collection process, with our 360-evaluation tools, evaluators should work with HR and each other to practice scoring evidence and to determine which types of evidence are most compelling.

Legal and policy issues present a possible complication. Policies vary from district to district concerning the kinds of information that can be included in an employee's evaluation. Consequently, some administrators may be more likely to use the tools we offer as resources in completing a coach's evaluation and not necessarily as the "evaluation form" itself. Regardless of how they intend to use these tools, before implementing them, administrators should communicate with human resources professionals, teachers' unions or other relevant professional associations, the school board, and coaches in their districts, as appropriate, to obtain any necessary approvals or required revisions.

EVIDENCE FOR EVALUATION

As pointed out earlier, completing our 360-evaluation forms is not as simple as "checking boxes." Deep evaluation processes require evidence. We must use evidence to inform actions and perceptions. Without evidence from the administrator to back up evaluation findings, coaches may be skeptical of the fairness of the evaluation process. And without evidence from coaches about their coaching practice, administrators may be skeptical of the validity of both the teacher feedback and the coach self-evaluation.

Coaches need data on their work with teachers and on their own growth as coaches. For the purposes of coach evaluation, therefore, we use two types of data: data that the coach collects on students for teacher use and data that the coach collects for improvement of the coach's own practice.

DATA COLLECTED ON STUDENTS

When engaged in Impact Cycle work with teachers, coaches collect data both to help the teacher set a goal for their students' improvement (the Identify phase) and to assist the teacher in tracking the goal until the students achieve it (the Improve phase) (Knight, 2017). In Impact Cycles, teachers set PEERS goals for their students in one or more of these three areas:

1. Academic achievement
(For example, "At least 85% of students will improve by 2 rubric points from their pretest scores on the concluding paragraph portion of the argumentative essay posttest.")

2. Student engagement
(For example, "All students will report themselves to be either strategically compliant or authentically engaged during five self-reported data collections on classroom activities.")

3. Positive learning environments/classroom management
(For example, "Students will transition to new activities in 2 minutes or less.")

Because PEERS goals are student-focused, the data on those goals not only serve to measure students' growth in the classroom but also the effectiveness of the coaching. That is, because the coach has supported the teacher in helping to set the goal, gathering data on the goal, and providing support follow-up on the goal, the students' success on the goal is also both the teacher's and the coach's success. Using goal data is a strong measure of the coach's impact with individual teachers and specific classrooms. The overall number of goals on which a coach is supporting teachers schoolwide can be a marker of his or her impact schoolwide as well.

Because the progress on PEERS goals is central to measuring their impact on student growth, coaches should have a process for tracking their goal progress with teachers that can be shared with their evaluators. That process should take into account the established boundaries of confidentiality for teachers, and the coach should collect artifacts or other information that assist the evaluator in understanding the data.

Our Impact Cycle Checklist (**Appendix 6**) can be a helpful start for coaches in deciding which elements of each cycle to track and what those data reports could look like. Two important elements to include are goals that coaches have set with teachers and the number of Impact Cycles started and achieved, but coaches should otherwise have flexibility in tracking various elements of their work with teachers to demonstrate that they are implementing the Seven Success Factors as fully as possible.

DATA COLLECTED ON COACHING PRACTICE

As the professionals whose jobs are most focused on the improvement of people in the school, coaches should collect data on their own practice so that they can also target areas of improvement for themselves. Depending on their role, their job expectations, and how they want to improve, coaches can collect data on coaching issues both at a macro level (What is my impact on schoolwide student data? Do teachers have a clear idea about what my job is and what a partnership approach is?) and a micro level (How well am I listening in coaching conversations? Am I tracking my time spent each day in a way that fully shows what I do? Am I better at data collection than data analysis?). As with the data that coaches collect for teachers, data on coaching practice should involve a consistent process and a sensitivity to the coaching confidentiality policy in the district.

Determining the kinds of data to track on coaching practice can be complicated and may evolve over time. When we first began our ICG Coaching Certification process, the question, "What evidence do we need coaches to provide that shows they're implementing the Seven Success Factors?" was at the forefront of our concerns. When Sharon coached teachers in the National Board Certification process in her school district, the National Board's candidate support provider training emphasized the desire for "clear, consistent, and convincing" evidence that teachers were accomplishing the standards. Easier said than done, perhaps. Some types of evidence are clearer than others, some types of evidence are more consistent than others, and some types are more convincing than others. Nevertheless, overall, for a given entry, scorers ask themselves, "Is the evidence clear, consistent, and convincing—and to what extent?"

As our first two candidate cohorts navigated the pilot iteration of the ICG Coaching Certification process, we modified the evidence pieces we requested. We reached out to a couple of colleagues from ETS in Princeton, NJ, for their suggestions on ways to improve our scoring procedures, and they helped us gain clarity about evidence. Specifically, they helped us to understand that

» some standards are more critical to success in a profession than other standards are, and
» some standards are easier to score objectively than other standards are.

To make scoring valid and reliable, our colleagues at ETS recommended that we consider focusing evidence pieces on the aspects of a job that are both

Our revised directions for certification candidates reflect our new thinking about evidence (see www.instructionalcoaching.com/certifications/develop-portfolio for the updated directions with evidence descriptions). Examining the evidence that we require for candidates could be the impetus for a conversation between evaluators and coaches about evidence that may be helpful in the employee evaluation process as well. For example, administrators and coaches should ask, "Which types of evidence of excellent coaching would be the most clear, consistent, and convincing in our context?"

BETTER FEEDBACK AND EVALUATION CONVERSATIONS

THE COMPLEXITIES OF PROVIDING FEEDBACK

One adult evaluating another adult automatically sets up the possibility of tension and resistance to feedback (Stone & Heen, 2014). Employers are duty-bound to identify and state problems with employee performance, and employees can easily feel maligned and misunderstood during those conversations. To avoid this dynamic, some evaluators try to move through the process as quickly and lightly as possible, merely going through the motions of the evaluation form. As Lee (2020), writing for SHRM, says, "When difficult information needs to be shared, managers may delay or avoid giving feedback" (p. 2).

As we have mentioned throughout, current evaluation forms are problematic in most of the coaching evaluation situations we've encountered, and so is the tendency to avoid or minimize the conversation around the coach's genuine needs for growth. For evaluation conversations to be truly helpful, they need to involve feedback and discussion around what coaching could be.

Lee (2020) defines feedback as "the exchange of information about the status and quality of work products" (p. 1). It can "motivate, support, direct, correct and regulate work efforts and outcomes and ensures that managers and employees are in sync and agree on the standards and expectations of the work to be performed" (p. 1). But, he explains, "feedback and performance appraisals are not one and the same" (p. 1). While evaluations are written, retrospective, and involve judgment on performance, feedback is often verbal, can be part of the annual evaluation but also can be more immediate (not solely tied to evaluation), and is sometimes perceived as less judgmental.

Because employee evaluations are "high stakes" for the employee, employees may react to the feedback they receive in evaluation conversations emotionally. As van Nieuwerburgh (2017) says, "If a teacher receives negative feedback about what she does, it is not reasonable to expect her not to take it personally" (p. 72). That's true for instructional coaches as well. Nonetheless, "to function at their best, coaches need to be able to receive feedback from others" (van Nieuwerburgh, 2017, p. 61). Giving feedback that the employee will be willing to hear is challenging but necessary.

BETTER FEEDBACK

Much has been written on the subject of feedback and evaluations, and people respond in their own ways to those kinds of conversations. Below are four guidelines for delivering feedback that can help those conversations to be more helpful for the coach and less anxiety-producing for everyone.

1. Provide ongoing and timely feedback.

2. Provide feedback on performance, not on ratings.

3. Provide feedback with intention and discretion.

4. Use tools from *Better Conversations* (Knight, 2016) to improve as a feedback conversation partner.

Provide ongoing and timely feedback.

Once-a-year feedback does not help employees grow as professionals. "Managers who rely on performance appraisals as their primary management tool are known to save up a year's worth of criticism and give it to the employee in one big dose at the annual performance evaluation, which may be catastrophic for some employees" (Lee, 2020, p. 2). Feedback, by definition, should be ongoing. What is true of an instructional coach in September may not be true in November, so feedback must be consistent with current performance to have any validity for the coach.

Ongoing feedback also supports the idea that the evaluator is a partner in the coach's improvement. "Periodic feedback sessions give the manager and employee multiple opportunities to calibrate and recalibrate their joint efforts. Like two paths diverging, the longer it takes between the time the manager and employee speak about a performance problem, the greater the distance will be between planned and actual performance improvement" (Lee, 2020, p. 1). Encouraging the coach to ask for feedback in specific areas further fosters a degree of partnership in the conversation and shows a respect for the employee's judgment and autonomy. In providing timely and ongoing feedback (and in being open to dialogue about those issues with the coach), the evaluator sends a clear message that they value the coach, are invested in the coach's work, and want to support the coach in every possible way.

Provide feedback on performance, not on ratings.

The fact that evaluation processes often involve forms with rating scales makes conversations about improvement challenging.

"Many people react to ratings rather than hearing the important information behind the ratings. Performance interventions must give the employee enough information about improvement points and the right amount of support to change them" (Lee, 2020, p. 2). That is, employees may naturally focus on "Why did I get this rating and not that rating?" in evaluation conversations.

To help coaches to be more open to discussing avenues for growth, focus not on rankings and scores but rather on their goals for the future as well as specific elements of their performance that they want to improve and others in which they take pride. Helping an employee to see the value in focusing on goals instead of rankings is challenging, just as it is to help students focus on areas for improvement instead of on their grades. But because the goals are the most helpful part of the evaluation to help the employee move forward, it is important for evaluators not to avoid the challenge.

Providing the coach with the written copy of the evaluation the day before the evaluation conversation can be helpful. Allowing coaches to read the form, the rankings, and any narratives in advance allows them the time and space to think about their responses before expressing their thoughts to their supervisor. Conveying the message that the evaluator sees employees as full human beings and not a score is central to engaging them in conversations about growth.

To focus more on performance and less on ratings, it is helpful to understand the difference between traditional feedback and dialogical feedback. Traditional feedback is feedback that advises a particular way of performing a task that involves little or no ambiguity. For example, when medical professionals learn to measure a patient's blood pressure, they need to follow exact steps (positioning the patient's limbs, the timing of the procedure, etc.) and the use of specific tools (a stethoscope and a sphygmomanometer). Any deviation from that procedure or those tools could result in a faulty measurement, an outcome that can have dire consequences. Medical personnel learning to perform that task benefit from direct advice on how to ensure they follow each step correctly every single time.

Dialogical feedback, on the other hand, involves a task at hand is quite complex and often not carried out the same way in every situation. In an environment as complex as a classroom, there is no "one right way" to do anything that will work for all students every time, so feedback should involve dialogue. For example, if a principal and a teacher both watch a video of the teacher's classroom, they can each contribute ideas about what is happening and options about how to improve it. No one should dictate a single course of action with all students. Dialogue encourages thinking of multiple paths to improvement and respects the employee as the one who decides how to move forward.

When providing coaches with feedback on their practice with teachers, this distinction is important, too. Coaching work is incredibly complex because of its emphasis on human interaction. Using data and evidence of coaching practice as a starting point for dialogue about how the coach is doing and what she can do in the future is more helpful than cut-and-dry statements about how things should be. Although evaluation may involve some cut-and-dry elements like rankings on a form, feedback conversations should be more dialogical, more growth-focused, and thus more helpful and inspiring for the coach.

Provide feedback with intention and discretion.
For the past three years, we have partnered with Growth Coaching International (GCI) in delivering their work and ours to schools worldwide. In our research involving districts who piloted our teacher, coach, and administrator forms for this book, one respondent from Texas who had attended one of our

GROWTH Coaching workshops suggested that "Administrators would benefit from understanding GROWTH Coaching when having evaluation conversations." We agree.

In fact, in chapter 7 of *The Leader's Guide to Coaching in Schools*, John Campbell and Christian van Nieuwerburgh of GCI provide specific guidance on feedback that both administrators and coaches may find particularly helpful. GCI categorizes feedback into three types:

1. **CONCERN-BASED FEEDBACK** (in which the evaluator addresses a specific and often serious concern about performance)

2. **LEARNING-BASED FEEDBACK** (in which the evaluator provides the employee with feedback as the employee learns something new)

3. **POSITIVE-BASED FEEDBACK** (in which the evaluator identifies all of the good things they see in the employee's performance) (Campbell & van Nieuwerburgh, 2018, pp. 79-90)

Because each of these types of feedback elicits a different response from employees, GCI recommends an intentional approach in deciding when to use each one:

1. **CONCERN-BASED FEEDBACK:** *use minimally*

2. **LEARNING-BASED FEEDBACK:** *use more often than concern-based but still judiciously*

3. **POSITIVE-BASED FEEDBACK:** *use all the time*

If employees receive a list of serious concerns about their performance, they are likely to shut down as listeners when hearing anything after the first item on the list. Addressing serious concerns in as focused a manner as possible involves more hope for employees that they can improve. While learning-based feedback may not involve the same kind of fear responses that concern-based feedback does, being careful and intentional in offering it can reinforce to employees that their supervisor views learning as a process and is not judging them. Finally, using positive-based feedback as often as possible shows employees that the evaluator sees them as full human beings with strengths and challenges, which makes them more open to hearing the evaluator's ideas.

In addition, Lee (2020) sees a connection between using discretion when offering feedback and the timeliness of feedback: "Supervisors can manage negative feedback by giving it in small, manageable doses. And when you give negative feedback during a feedback session vs. at an annual appraisal, the employee has the opportunity and time to digest the information and make corrections" (p. 2).

Because they are such committed professionals, some supervisors may think, "Our coaches want our feedback. They ask for it all the time, so I don't need to tiptoe around them like I do other employees." Resisting feedback (even when we've asked for it) is as normal for humans as inhaling oxygen and exhaling carbon dioxide (Stone & Heen, 2014). Coaches need the same care and consideration in feedback conversations as anyone else does. Evaluations are inherently "high stakes" for every employee, and creating humanizing feedback conversations for coaches fosters that kind of professional culture for everyone in a school.

Feedback delivered well can build relationships "because when major challenges are presented, the environment of dialogue—and hopefully trust—is already established. This makes it easier to discuss and deal with real issues when they occur" (Lee, 2020, p. 2).

Use the beliefs and habits of *Better Conversations* to improve as a conversation partner.

We believe that, when in doubt, partnership is the best way to handle challenging situations. Lee (2020) agrees regarding feedback conversations tied to evaluation: "The best way to find solutions to common problems is to collaborate, and this collaboration requires conversation" (p. 1). Full partnership is not necessarily possible in a supervisor-employee relationship, but the more the leader seeks to create a partnership-like environment, the safer the employee will feel to be honest and vulnerable in those discussions, and the more likely the employee is to be open to the thoughts of his or her supervisor.

Traditional evaluation conversations are top-down in nature. That is, the evaluator ranks the employee on the evaluation tool, the evaluator's voice is the dominant one in the discussion, and the employee may sense an expectation to respond positively and minimally to what the evaluator says. If that dynamic worked, it would surely be easier on everyone—and time saving—but historically it hasn't worked. Instead, it leaves employees feeling misunderstood, undervalued, and voiceless.

Conversations that encourage the coach's voice and ideas take time, and developing an improvement plan takes time. If the evaluation process is to result in real, self-driven change for the coach, it is crucial not only to provide time for that to happen but also to approach the coach as a partner in change.

Better evaluation conversations involve the coach speaking as much as the evaluator. In fact, if the evaluator is willing to put aside the administrator form and its rankings and instead use the coach's self-evaluation form to drive the conversation, the coach will feel much safer to engage and elaborate on what coaching looks like and how the coach wants to improve. Encouraging and supporting employee engagement and voice means changing the traditional dynamics of evaluation conversations. To do that means undoing habits like focusing on rankings and evaluator observations and placing the emphasis on the coach's ideas first.

In Jim's book *Better Conversations* (Knight, 2016), he offers a framework for thinking about how to improve personal and professional communication based on the findings of research he did with more than 1,000 participants. The resulting six *Better Conversations* Beliefs are dispositions that help us to focus on specific aspects of conversations to increase the spirit of partnership with others. For evaluators in feedback conversations or other discussions around the evaluation process, four of those beliefs may be most helpful to think about when preparing for evaluation conversations:

» I want to hear what others have to say.
» I don't judge others.
» Conversation should be back and forth.
» Conversation should be life-giving.

With these beliefs in mind, administrators can more effectively self-monitor their responses in the conversation. For example, instead of thinking, "How can we end this conversation sooner?," the administrator will wonder, "What does the coach need from me right now? How can I best show support and encourage her voice in these matters?" or "Is this the right time to address [insert evaluator concern]?" instead of assuming that whatever the evaluator wants to discuss is what should be on the table.

In focusing on these beliefs, we're asking school and district leaders to "flip the script" on what they may perceive as the leadership stance in an evaluation situation. We believe this important because by actively seeking to withhold judgment on what coaches are saying, by encouraging their voice in the form of a dialogue about where they want to improve and how they might do that, the evaluator shows genuine concern for the coach and a belief that the coach can improve and achieve excellence.

Because an "evaluation" process is naturally conferring a "judgment" on the coach, a leader may understandably wonder, "How can I evaluate without judging?" It is true that while evaluation processes may require some summative judgments, the leader can still create an environment where coaches feel safe to say what they think about the forms and the process, about their performance, and about their plan for improvement. Withholding judgment as much as possible in those conversations helps the evaluator avoid interrupting, becoming defensive, and inadvertently silencing the coach as a result. "When you remove judgment from feedback, [employees are] more likely to receive information in the spirit in which it was intended" (Lee, 2020, p. 2). Sharing evidence versus sharing judgment with the coach keeps the conversation focused on performance, not on personality or perceived "attacks."

In addition to the beliefs, *Better Conversations* (Knight, 2016) also offers 10 *Better Conversations* Habits that can be used to set goals in communication to try to "walk the talk" of the beliefs. On the *Better Conversations* resources page, readers can download forms that they can use to reflect on how well they are implementing the habits in conversation and subsequently develop a plan for how to improve in habits they choose (see https://resources.corwin.com/knightbetterconversations). Habits that may be of particular interest to evaluators who want to improve their evaluation and feedback conversations include

» Demonstrating Empathy,
» Listening With Empathy,
» Fostering Dialogue,
» Being a Witness to the Good, and
» Asking Better Questions.

Each of these habits can be helpful in working to withhold judgment and to encourage coaches to voice their ideas in the conversation. Sometimes, despite everyone's best intentions, evaluation conversations become tense, uncomfortable, confrontational, or just plain unhelpful. If the evaluator anticipates that maintaining a better conversation may be problematic in a particular situation, focusing on three other habits may be helpful to navigate those tensions:

» Finding Common Ground,
» Controlling Toxic Emotions, and
» Redirecting Toxic Conversations.

Administrators have a great deal of power in creating evaluation environments that are humanizing, life-giving, and focused on hope and growth. Such environments rarely happen by accident. Focusing on improving their approach to evaluation is crucial for employers who want coaches to have a similar feeling of empowerment and agency over their own professional practice.

ılılı

Despite the pervasive issues of lack of role clarity, use of evaluation forms that are not focused on coaching, and the other legal, ethical, and interpersonal issues surrounding evaluation of employees, one thing is constant: Wherever we go, school and district leaders are vocal and enthusiastic about how much they value their instructional coaches. We agree: Coaches are overwhelmingly hardworking, positive, intelligent, capable, student-focused, kind people.

Ironically, perhaps part of the reason why coaching evaluation has been neglected to date relates to how much coaches are valued as employees. Regardless of what evaluation paradigm they're in, evaluators value their coaches and will make sure that coaches don't suffer negative consequences because of faulty evaluation forms, and coaches will likely be patient and cheerful about the situation.

But we want more. We want an evaluation process that acknowledges the complex and challenging work that coaches do to support teachers and students. We want a process that is fair, clear, and tied to best coaching practices. We want a process that focuses on improvement for the most important improvement specialists in the school. We want what coaches deserve—the best we can do to measure and honor the work they do every day.

 # To Sum Up

- » Understanding the research-based Seven Success Factors of effective coaching programs is key in aligning evaluation processes with coaching best practices.

- » A 360-evaluation approach is helpful for instructional coaches because so much of their work depends on the quality of their interactions with others. Feedback from teachers, in particular, is crucial to obtain data on how effective coaching is. Implementing a 360-evaluation approach can involve some of the complexities that we mention in this chapter regarding the perception of fairness, the challenges of teacher's union contract negotiations, and so on. To do 360-evaluation well involves engaging all stakeholders in developing a process that is fair and feasible for everyone.

- » Understanding which types of evidence provide the clearest, most consistent, and most convincing evidence of effective coaching is essential in creating valid and reliable evaluation tools.

- » Using the tools from *Better Conversations* (Knight, 2016) and GROWTH Coaching (Campbell & van Nieuwerburgh, 2018) can aid evaluators in creating feedback and evaluation environments in which coaches feel safe to use their voice and set goals for their own improvement.

Making It Real

To make effective coach evaluation real, examine the teacher, coach, and administrator forms provided in the Appendix. Would including these forms in your evaluation process be a natural extension of how coaching works in your school or district, or is lack of role clarity such a key issue that it needs to be examined at the school or district level before these kinds of questions can be included in the process? If so, then delving into that element before making judgments about evaluation is time well spent.

⊙ Reflection Questions

What was most valuable in this chapter?

....

....

....

....

....

Which elements of research-based instructional coaching are evident in your current coach job description and evaluation system?

....

....

....

....

....

....

Which elements of research-based coaching would you like to add to your evaluation system?

....

....

....

....

....

Which types of data or evidence would you want to see as part of a coach's evaluation process?

....

....

....

....

....

....

Would the teacher, coach, and administrator forms be helpful in aligning your evaluation process with research-based coaching? What would you modify or add?

....

....

....

....

....

Do you need to improve the style or content of your evaluation and feedback conversations?

....

....

....

....

....

....

The 360-evaluation process makes some leaders nervous because they involve multiple employees contributing to the evaluation of others. When implementing any 360-style process, evaluators should thoroughly investigate their organization's human resources policies regarding those kinds of structures and ensure that they strictly follow existing guidelines. In addition, reaching out to teachers' unions as partners early in the process of creating a fair 360 evaluation is crucial in ensuring that all stakeholders have confidence in coach evaluation. Respecting existing teacher contracts and regulations is central to a process that employees find to be engaging and humanizing versus punitive and demoralizing.

The Society for Human Resource Management (SHRM) provides a great deal of research and resources on employee evaluation that may also be helpful. We've cited several of their publications throughout this book, but two pieces specific to 360 evaluation can help evaluators navigate potential complications. Joan Lloyd (2009) describes the potential benefits of a 360-evaluation approach as a leadership tool, while Steve Taylor (2011) discusses the pros and cons of using 360 evaluation to help evaluators make sound decisions in implementing it.

The use of feedback in evaluation conversations can present challenges for both evaluators and employees. In addition to the feedback guidelines we described from GCI (Campbell & van Nieuwerburgh, 2018), Douglas Stone and Sheila Heen's (2014) *Thanks for the Feedback* examines in depth the psychological complexities of feedback to help professionals become more adept at giving feedback and less resistant to hearing feedback from others. Their helpful road map provides a process for evaluators to reflect on their feedback practices and prepare to give feedback in various situations.

The work of teaching, coaching, leading, and learning is critical, and that means that leaders must be continually reflective about how they evaluate, what they evaluate, and which evaluation practices work best.

CHAPTER 3

EVALUATING INSTRUCTIONAL COACHING PROGRAMS

is about

creating a process
for evaluating whether
instructional coaching
programs are positively
affecting student
growth

*by determining
a process for*

by acknowledging

Measuring
success at
the program
level

System
responsibility
for coaching
success

- Using the Seven Success Factors to guide program evaluation

- An instructional coaching program audit

- Importance of communication

- Why system support matters

- What system support looks like

03

///

EVALUATING INSTRUCTIONAL COACHING

PROGRAMS

 SNAPSHOT:

This chapter describes our suggestions for creating

an evaluation process for an instructional coaching

program, including guidance on how to conduct an

audit to measure program success. You can skip this

chapter and move to chapter 4 if you are focused more

on individual coaches as employees and want to learn

about recruiting and hiring instructional coaches.

Reshma loved being a teacher but decided many years ago to become a principal and, later, a district-level administrator. She became an administrator because she wanted to ensure that teachers received effective instructional support so that they could, in turn, more effectively support student learning.

As the director of elementary education in her district, Reshma saw the need to move past "one-and-done" professional development (PD) sessions to ensure lasting change. She envisioned a deeper kind of professional learning for the teachers, one that differentiated what they were focusing on and implementing according to the needs of their students. She wanted teachers to feel empowered to make positive change for students and reverse the common sentiment that PD is something "done to" teachers, not something done in partnership with them.

Reshma read Jim's books *Instructional Coaching* (Knight, 2007) and *The Impact Cycle* (Knight, 2017) and saw the benefits of changing her district's traditional top-down approach to professional learning, which had long looked something like this:

"OK, teachers. Here's your problem. Here's a new program/strategy to show you how to fix it. Now go and use it exactly the way we say to use it. We'll be in periodically to make sure you're doing it right."

She thought teachers would be more engaged in change with a partnership approach that positioned them as decision-makers:

"What concerns do you have about your students right now? What would you like to see them doing differently? What strategy would you like to use to make that change? How should we measure their progress? How can I assist you in the plan?"

She consulted with Jim, and together they developed a coaching program structure in which coaches would work with any teacher who requested support in working on their goals for their students. After communicating with teachers about the program and establishing clear parameters for the coaches about how to use their time, Reshma saw that an increasing number of teachers were asking to work with the coaches, including teachers in all grade levels and content areas and with differing levels of experience.

Principals became engaged in coaching too, and asked coaches to help them learn some of the programs and strategies that the teachers were using. Coaches maintained a clear confidentiality policy with teachers, and teacher feedback on coaching was very positive. System planning benefited as well because the coaches were able to use their experience in classrooms to have conversations with district leaders about professional development needs for teachers as a whole. In short, Reshma did everything right in establishing a coaching program that very likely would show student improvement.

Nonetheless, when annual county budget battles began again in January of the coaching program's second year, cuts to the education budget were looming. As with any sizeable organization, making large-scale cuts to a public school budget typically means cutting jobs because so much of the school budget is invested in personnel. When the school board approached Reshma about the 40 instructional coaching positions she had created, they had questions:

> » Exactly what does a coach do?
>
> » Can you show us data that demonstrate the impact of coaching on students?

Despite all of her good planning, Reshma had not foreseen the need to educate the board about coaching in the way she had been communicating about the role with teachers and school leaders. In addition, although she had some data on teacher response and the impact of coaching on teaching practices, she had no system in place to track student growth and impact. In short, the school board couldn't see the value of coaching because they didn't understand it, and the district had no data from coaching that they could tie directly to students. To make the mandated budget cuts, the school board cut all 40 coaching positions.

Reshma was crushed. She saw the program making a difference in so many classrooms. She saw how hard the coaches worked to engage teachers as partners. "Had they given me a little more time," she thought, "I could have shown them what they asked to see. But now it's all gone."

PROFESSIONAL LEARNING VERSUS PROFESSIONAL DEVELOPMENT

Throughout this chapter, we use the terms *professional development* and *professional learning*. We believe that distinguishing between those terms is important.

PROFESSIONAL DEVELOPMENT:

Activities that may or may not lead to professional learning; they typically focus on perceived teacher deficits, are "one size fits all," and focus on the expertise of the facilitator

PROFESSIONAL LEARNING:

Professional growth experiences that focus on student needs, are "one size fits one," and involve teachers as learners and leaders

We hear stories like Reshma's all the time. Instructional coaching programs are subject to the same threats to sustainability as anything else in education (budget cuts, leadership changes, competing initiatives, and so on). But there are ways to protect them. Because coaching has the power to significantly change classroom instruction, consistently evaluating coaching programs has two purposes that are important in serving students well:

1. Program evaluation provides valuable information about the impact of the coaching to make the best decisions about how to continuously improve the coaching program from year to year.

2. Program evaluation data can arm leaders with proof that the investment in personnel, coaching training, and time is worth the results to sustain coaching positions and programs in schools.

But, evaluating coaching programs presents some of the same reasons as evaluating instructional coaches as employees (as described in chapter 2)—how to define *instructional coaching*, problems with role clarity, and confusion over how coaches should spend their time at school.

In this chapter, we discuss how to use some of the tools from chapter 2 to evaluate coaching programs, how to conduct an instructional coaching program audit, and why embracing a broader view of who is responsible for coaching success is essential. Our goal is to provide schools and districts with the tools they need to demonstrate the impact of coaching on teachers and students so that they can sustain instructional coaching programs as a critical and continuing part of professional learning.

Measuring Success at the Program Level

Professional learning has long been recognized as a key part of school improvement. Joellen Killion (2018) explains that, "To increase capacity, education leaders at the state, district, and school levels invest in professional learning" (p. xiii). According to Killion, the purpose of evaluating professional learning is to determine "whether a particular program has merit, worth, value, and impact," and the use of data to determine the program's current state can be helpful in informing future program decisions.

Killion (2018) shares Thomas Guskey's (2000) definition of evaluation: Evaluating professional learning does not refer solely to measuring the success of "event-based" PD (e.g., workshops, professional days) but also to measuring ongoing, daily forms of professional learning such as instructional coaching. Guskey acknowledges that many school districts evaluate their professional learning programs to some extent but points to three mistakes that districts commonly make when doing so:

Evaluations often focus on documentation rather than a thorough review of a program's successes and needs. In other words, program evaluations involve data collection but not the deep data analysis that leads to changes for improvement.

1.   Evaluations are often shallow and do not address meaningful indicators of success.

2.   Evaluations are too brief and extend over too short a time period for the evaluation results to be valid and reliable (Guskey, 2000).

In our work with school districts, we also see Guskey's three concerns in coaching program evaluation. Specifically,

1. Coaching program evaluation may focus on whether training was delivered to coaches but not on whether coaches actually fully implemented the Impact Cycle (Knight, 2017) and/or not on whether those cycles had an impact on student growth.

2. Coaching program evaluation is not typically tied to an aspirational set of coaching standards or a rubric, which makes the path forward more difficult to chart and less likely to inspire coaches to want to improve.

3. Coaching program evaluation may only consider data points in the current school year as opposed to trends over time. Deep change for teachers and school communities takes time, and data collection needs to happen over time to capture the full picture of coaching impact in the building.

Professional learning programs involve many stakeholders, so determining the information that is most helpful in evaluating those programs can be difficult. That work is important not only to make decisions about the programs themselves but also to ensure the engagement of employees in them. As Dennis Sparks argues in the Foreword to Guskey's book *Evaluating Professional Development* (2000), "Teachers want to know if staff development is making their work more effective and efficient, and particularly whether improvements in students learning justify the often-difficult changes they are being asked to make" (p. xi). Evaluating programs in a way that is "thoughtful, intentional, and purposeful" (Guskey, 2000, p. 42) and sharing the evaluation results with transparency gives everyone more confidence that professional learning experiences are moving schools forward.

Providing high-quality professional learning experiences and resources to teachers has an important effect on school culture. In Jim's books *Unmistakable Impact* (Knight, 2011) and *High-Impact Instruction* (Knight, 2013), he describes the characteristics of what he refers to as Impact Schools—schools in which "every aspect of professional learning is designed to have an unmistakable, positive impact on teaching and, hence, student learning" (Knight, 2011, p. 6). He identifies the four pillars of Impact Schools (Knight, 2013):

1.   Professional learning must embody respect for the professionalism of teachers by involving teachers as true partners in their professional learning.

2.   Professional learning should provide a clear focus for sustained growth, and teachers should be collaborators on the school improvement plan.

3.   Teachers should have sufficient support with the implementation of new practices.

4.   Coaches, principals, educational leaders, and teachers need a deep knowledge of *High-Impact Instructional* strategies that have a significant, positive impact on students' behavior, attitudes, engagement, and learning.

When we create environments of respect, goal setting, appropriate support, and high-quality professional learning, we create cultures of improvement that permeate all aspects of the school. Susan Rosenholz's work in the area of school culture reinforces the benefits of creating deep learning environments not only for students but also for teachers: "The primary psychic rewards for most teachers come from students' academic accomplishments—from feeling certain about their own capacity to affect student growth and development. Indeed, teacher certainty about professional practice—their sense of efficacy about pedagogical skills—and student achievement are very highly correlated and professional certainty is positively related to teachers' decisions to remain teaching" (Rosenholtz, 1985, pp. 355-356).

But working toward establishing those four pillars is not enough. Measuring the extent to which they are in place and what student growth looks like as a result is critical in fostering the school community's belief in its professional culture as one that serves everyone.

Even though some of the issues are similar, as pointed out earlier, evaluating instructional coaching programs is in some ways less complicated than evaluating instructional coaches (as described in chapter 2). For example, evaluating programs does not involve as many legal or human resources issues as evaluating employees does. Nonetheless, to evaluate the impact of a program and determine its future directions requires a process.

Mark Dowley, director of staff development and instruction at Brighton Grammar School in Brighton, Victoria, Australia, uses Kirkpatrick and *Kirkpatrick's Four Levels of Training Evaluation* (2016) when examining professional learning in his school. Mark spoke to Jim about that process (M. Dowley, personal communication, May 26, 2020). The Kirkpatrick model involves examination of four facets of professional learning experiences (Kirkpatrick & Kirkpatrick, 2016):

» "**LEVEL 1:** Reaction: The degree to which participants find the training favorable, engaging and relevant to their jobs
» **LEVEL 2:** Learning: The degree to which participants acquire the intended knowledge, skills, attitude, confidence and commitment based on their participation in the training
» **LEVEL 3:** Behavior: The degree to which participants apply what they learned during training when they are back on the job
» **LEVEL 4:** Results: The degree to which targeted outcomes occur as a result of the training and the support and accountability package" (p. 10)

Mark describes his school's use of the four levels to evaluate instructional coaching, as follows:

> [W]e first started the program, and we worked for six teachers. We used the Kirkpatrick framework, which is a quick measure of the impact of training, essentially: Was it relevant? Did I learn something new? Did I apply that? And did it have an impact on students?
>
> We had a number of different avenues for professional learning. One of them was peer coaching, another was instructional coaching, yet another was whole-school presentations, and involved external professional development. We asked the teachers who were in the coaching program to write where they were on that scale and which type of professional learning was the most effective ... instructional coaching was through the roof.

Having a consistent evaluation process in place aids Mark and other school leaders in making the best decisions about professional learning. "I think that one of the key things that's helped the program develop is making sure that it's still working and making changes. We've made tweaks and changes every six months, every term, and it's quite an adaptive process as it's grown." The data they have from the evaluation process also back Mark in sustaining and expanding the school's coaching program. "I can go to my boss or school leadership and say, 'Look, this is the money we've invested in coaching. It's actually having the biggest impact on students out of all of these things. So the data are showing that coaching is worth the investment, and that data is an important piece in developing and sustaining the program each year.'"

Mark's school also brought in an external consultant to review their coaching documentation and to interview 20 members of the staff about coaching. At the end of that review process, the consultant submitted a report that said, "The process left me in no doubt the Coaching Program is and will continue to improve teacher pedagogy and student outcomes" (M. Dowley, personal communication, May 26, 2020).

School and district administrators want to do the right thing for students and for staff. But financial considerations and competing agendas are always problematic in deciding what the "right" things are at any given time, so having a process that provides good data for making those decisions benefits everyone.

Joellen Killion (2018), Thomas Guskey (2000), and the James and Wendy Kirkpatrick (2016) are all important voices in the professional learning field, and we recommend their texts as resources for creating the best possible evaluation process for your professional learning programs. Because our work is instructional coaching, the next section of this chapter will describe a framework for evaluating instructional coaching programs specifically.

USING THE SEVEN SUCCESS FACTORS TO GUIDE PROGRAM EVALUATION
To ensure a sound evaluation process that aids the school district in determining the worth and merit of the program, Guskey (2000) uses a four-part process to evaluate programs:

1. Determine standards for judging quality.

2. Decide whether those standards should be relative or absolute.

3. Collect relevant information.

4. Apply the standards to determine value or quality.

These steps mirror our approach to evaluation and can serve as a checklist as you create your own evaluation process. That is, we recommend that school districts approach program evaluation by

1.   using our Standards and Quality Indicators (Appendix 1) as the aspirational markers of coaching success,

2.   comparing those standards and indicators to what their coaches do to determine any changes that are necessary in the evaluation process or in their coaching roles,

3.   determining the types of data and evidence that demonstrate performance against the Standards and Quality Indicators, and

4.   using the data and evidence to make judgments about performance that also can shape goals for improvement.

 ## PLANNING A COACHING PROGRAM EVALUATION PROCESS CHECKLIST

EVALUATING INSTRUCTIONAL COACHES	☑
Use our Standards and Quality Indicators (Appendix 1) as the aspirational markers of coaching success.	○
Compare those standards and indicators to what their coaches do to determine any changes that are necessary in the evaluation process or in their coaching roles.	○
Determine the types of data and evidence that demonstrate performance against the Standards and Quality Indicators.	○
Use the data and evidence to make judgments about performance that also can shape goals for improvement.	○

Those four elements of coaching evaluation apply equally to evaluating coaches as employees (chapter 2) or evaluating coaching programs. We next describe how to create program evaluation tools using the Kirkpatricks' four elements as our guide.

STEP 1: USE THE STANDARDS AND QUALITY INDICATORS

When determining what to include in program evaluation, the Seven Success Factors for Effective Coaching Programs (Knight, 2021) provide the most helpful, research-based framework for schools:

» **FACTOR ONE:** Partnership Principles
» **FACTOR TWO:** The Impact Cycle
» **FACTOR THREE:** Data
» **FACTOR FOUR:** Instructional Playbook
» **FACTOR FIVE:** Communication Habits and Skills
» **FACTOR SIX:** Leadership
» **FACTOR SEVEN:** System Support

Each of the factors is described in more detail in chapter 2. As with the evaluation of instructional coaches, we recommend using the Standards and Quality Indicators in Appendix 1 as the coaching program's standards of excellence, too, thereby ensuring that the evaluation is aligned with research-based best practices for instructional coaching. Such alignment is important because defining success in the same way for individual coaches and for coaching programs does three things:

1. It establishes a system-wide definition of *instructional coaching*.

2. It helps to ensure role clarity for instructional coaches.

3. It makes connecting individual coaches' performance to program performance easier for leaders.

Once leaders have decided to use the Standards and Quality Indicators for program evaluation, the next step involves comparing them to the goals and parameters of the coaching program.

STEP 2: COMPARE THE STANDARDS AND QUALITY INDICATORS TO WHAT COACHES DO

Leaders should next examine the Quality Indicators for each standard (Appendix 1) to determine which elements of a particular success factor are most important to evaluate in their context. By examining the elements of coaching programs from a district perspective (and ideally including school-based administrators and coaches in that process), districts can further surface issues surrounding role clarity and time that they may need to address (as described in chapters 1 and 2).

Our Standards and Quality Indicators may not encompass everything that coaches do in a given district or everything that leaders consider part of coaching program success. We generally recommend that coaches spend most of their school time (60-70%) working with teachers in Impact Cycle goals to have an impact school-wide (Thomas, 2018a). That leaves potentially 30-40% of their work time for other duties that may be important as part of the program evaluation. Scrutinizing those roles to determine which ones have a student impact or schoolwide impact versus those that do not is helpful in gathering data specific to evaluate program success.

STEP 3: DETERMINE TYPES OF DATA AND EVIDENCE THAT DEMONSTRATE PERFORMANCE

Once leaders have determined which aspects of the Standards they want to evaluate, how to measure those Quality Indicators is next. Some of the data and evidence from coach evaluation (such as the 360-evaluation tools we describe in Appendices 3, 4, and 5) can also be a part of coaching program evaluation (to the extent that prevailing law and human resources policies permit that). If data from individual coaches' employee evaluations are used as part of the program evaluation, it is important to ensure that they are anonymized to protect the confidentiality of the employees. Because examining program concerns is broader than a single coach, however, other types of data and evidence are often essential.

"Because professional learning programs are situated within a context that influences the choice of intervention, its implementation, and most likely its results, evaluators consider carefully how to increase objectivity in their work to provide honest, reliable evaluations that will be useful" (Killion, 2018, p. 11). Data on coaching program success are just as important as data on coach performance, and choosing the best and most relevant data points is vital. Guskey (2000) reinforces the need for reliable and clear data: "Although no evaluation can be completely objective, the process is not based on opinion or conjecture" (p. 42).

The following data pieces are most helpful in evaluating coaching success:

» Number of PEERS goals that coaches have set and achieved with teachers (including copies of the goals and data tracking their progress)
» Number of Impact Cycles that coaches and teachers have started and the number of cycles completed
» A time log demonstrating that coaches are spending the majority of their time at school working in Impact Cycles with teachers
» Feedback from teachers that attests to both the coaches' partnership approach and the implementation of the Impact Cycle

To demonstrate the impact of instructional coaching on students, the most important data point on this list is the first: the number of PEERS goals that coaches have set and hit with teachers. Because PEERS goals focus on student improvement and not on teacher improvement, they are the data that most clearly show the coach's impact on students (see chapter 2 for more information on and examples of PEERS goals). PEERS goals involve specific criteria and a data-gathering process that tracks the change in students over time, from baseline to hitting the goal. We have seen goals labeled as PEERS that do not meet the PEERS criteria, and we have seen data indicating that goals were met but do not clearly show progress over time. These inconsistencies are problematic for measuring coaching success.

Coaches and evaluators must ensure that everyone is working from the same understanding of what PEERS goals are and how to collect data on them to ensure the date are valid and reliable. For example, school and district leaders can make discussing progress on PEERS goals a part of their regular meetings to ensure clear communication about goals and how to track them.

No magic number of goals or magic percentage of goals hit exists as a success threshold for coaching because coaching roles differ widely from place to place. Teachers set goals of differing scope, differing levels of difficulty, and differing time frames, and those factors alone make a magic number impossible. For example, when Michelle was an instructional coach, she coached teachers in all grade levels and content areas in her school. When Sharon was an instructional coach, she primarily worked with English teachers and only occasionally with teachers outside of English. Michelle and Sharon would have had very different numbers of goals each school year because Sharon worked with a significantly smaller coaching audience. The success marker that is more helpful for evaluators is growth in the number of goals set and hit from year to year. Growth over time would show increasing trust in coaches and an increasing focus on improvement within the school culture.

The teacher feedback, coach self-evaluation, and administrator forms provided in chapter 2 can provide useful information on the numbers of PEERS goals set and achieved, the numbers of Impact Cycles started and completed, and teachers' perceptions of the coaches' partnership approach. In chapter 2, we cautioned against including space on the teacher feedback form for narrative or anecdotal information to avoid legal issues around employee evaluation. When evaluating the overall coaching program, however, leaders can ask teachers to provide more detailed responses about their experiences with coaches since that evaluation is not focused on a particular employee. All three forms may be useful for program evaluation, but evaluators may also want other evidence to confirm the data on those forms.

Our ICG Coaching Certification process describes other forms of evidence that districts may want to consider in the evaluation (see https://www.instructionalcoaching.com/downloads/pdfs/ Certification/20-21_Portfolio_Directions_ICG-Certfication.pdf). For example, other data could include (but are not limited to)

» Data-tracking tools that coaches use to track Impact Cycles in progress
» Actual student work that coaches and teachers collect during Impact Cycles
» Any periodic teacher feedback assessments that coaches may have collected throughout the year
» Data on coaching that school administrators may keep on various aspects of student growth (in achievement, engagement, and/or classroom behavior) and school culture

STEP 4: USE DATA TO MAKE JUDGMENTS ABOUT PERFORMANCE AND TO SHAPE GOALS FOR IMPROVEMENT

In evaluating coach data and the evidence pieces, a rubric is helpful both to gauge progress and to set future goals for improvement. **Appendix 7** provides a modified version of our ICG Certification rubric specifically for instructional coaching programs that evaluators can use for this purpose ("Scoring Look-Fors": https://www.instructional-coaching.com/downloads/pdfs/Certification/20-21-Scoring-Look-Fors.pdf). The rubric aligns closely with the rubric for evaluating instructional coaches (Appendix 2) so that districts can use elements of individual coach evaluations as part of the program evaluation with a common frame of reference for success.

Once evaluators have determined how they want to use elements of the coach evaluation process to inform evaluation of the coaching program, they may next want to develop a structure for the evaluation process. The next section is a description of what an instructional coaching program audit can look like as part of evaluating coaching.

To aid districts in developing a similar evaluation process, use Form A to examine the most important parts of the program evaluation.

PROGRAM EVALUATION DEVELOPMENT FORM

///////////////

DEVELOP THE AUDIT CONTENT:

STEP 1: Use the Standards and Quality Indicators

Use the standards and quality indicators in Appendix 1 as the coaching program's standards of excellence.

» Which standards are the most helpful or relevant for your instructional coaching program evaluation?

» Have those standards you selected been clearly communicated to and discussed with all coaching stakeholders before evaluating them?

STEP 2: Compare the Standards and Quality Indicators to What Coaches Do

Examine the quality indicators for each standard (Appendix 1) to see which elements of a particular success factor are most important to evaluate in your context.

» Which quality indicators are the most helpful or relevant for your instructional coaching program evaluation?

» Will other coaching tasks outside of the quality indicators be measured to determine program success? Create quality indicators for those tasks.

» Have all of the quality indicators you selected been clearly communicated to and discussed with all coaching stakeholders before evaluating them?

STEP 3: Determine Types of Data and Evidence That Demonstrate Performance

Determine how to measure the Quality Indicators you selected. The following data pieces are most helpful in evaluating coaching success:

» Number of PEERS goals that coaches have set and achieved with teachers

» Number of Impact Cycles that coaches and teachers have started and the number of cycles completed

» A time log demonstrating that coaches are spending the majority of their time at school working in Impact Cycles with teachers

» Feedback from teachers that attests to both the coaches' partnership approach and to the implementation of the Impact Cycle

» How will you measure each Quality Indicator you selected?

» Which types of evidence will be most helpful to track progress for each?

» Have all of the data points and evidence pieces you selected been clearly communicated to and discussed with all coaching stakeholders before evaluating them?

STEP 4: Use Data to Make Judgments About Performance and to Shape Goals for Improvement

Examine our rubric for evaluating instructional coaching programs in Appendix 7.

» Which elements of the rubric will you use in your program evaluation?

» How should you structure the evaluation to ensure that every element is aligned with research and with best practices in evaluation?

» How will you communicate the evaluation purpose and process to all coaching stakeholders before evaluation begins?

AN INSTRUCTIONAL COACHING PROGRAM AUDIT

Recently, we completed our first coaching program audit process at the request of the leaders in Katy Independent School District (Katy ISD) in Katy, TX. Audits can be somewhat distinct from annual program evaluations in that they typically involve more people in the process and have a scope that may include multiple years' worth of program data. After having coaching positions in place for more than a decade but with coaches taking on varying roles and approaches across the district along the way, Katy ISD wanted to determine what's working, what's not working, and what their future direction should be. Because they had worked with Ann and Jim on learning and implementing our Impact Cycle coaching model as well as creating an Instructional Playbook, they invited ICG to partner with them to create an audit process to help them meet those goals (Instructional Coaching Group, 2020). This section provides a description of what that process looked like to help other districts visualize how all the elements of evaluation can come together as a whole.

THE AUDIT PROCESS

Katy ISD leaders first met with Ann and Jim to discuss their needs for an evaluation and to help Ann and Jim gather information about the existing coaching program. The ICG team then created an audit proposal that was submitted to those leaders. After some revisions, the audit began. The Katy ISD coaching audit included three phases of data collection and then a one-day presentation on the results to Katy ISD leaders. The data collection phases looked like this:

1. ICG staff created surveys that Katy ISD distributed to all teachers, coaches, and administrators who had experienced coaching within the past two years. Katy ISD modified the forms to address particular district nuances. (The surveys were an early iteration of the teacher, coach, and administrator forms described in chapter 2.)

2. ICG staff conducted focus group interviews at the Katy ISD campuses with more than 150 educational leaders. The focus groups were recorded and transcribed for analysis using qualitative analysis software to identify trends and themes.

3. ICG staff then conducted interviews at the office of the superintendent as well as the executive leadership team and other

leaders in the district. These interviews were also recorded and transcribed for analysis using qualitative analysis software to identify trends and themes.

In all, over 1,870 teachers and more than 200 principals and coaches submitted responses. ICG made the survey data available to all parties. Some of the observations from survey analysis include the following:

» Coaches, principals, and teachers nearly unanimously agreed that teachers were treated as partners, and dialogue was encouraged between coach and teacher (versus giving advice or directives).

» Principals generally believed that more checklists and playbooks were used than coaches and teachers did.

» Teachers reported a lesser degree of partnership when working with coaches in Impact Cycles (Knight, 2017) than principals and coaches reported.

» Coaches and principals reported more frequent partnering of coaches with teachers to problem solve than teachers did.

» Coaches and principals reported more frequent offering of choices to teachers regarding which high-impact strategies to use for their goals than teachers did.

With these results in hand, the leaders and coaches in Katy ISD are now targeting goals for improvement in various aspects of their coaching program and have solid program-wide data on which to develop paths toward those goals.

To aid in developing a similar audit process, districts may use Form B to examine the most important parts of a program audit.

PROGRAM AUDIT DEVELOPMENT FORM

////////////////

Make Initial Decisions:

» What is the purpose of this audit, and how will you use the data you collect?

» Inside auditor or outside auditor?

» What is the scope of this audit?

DEVELOP THE AUDIT CONTENT:

STEP 1: Use the Standards and Quality Indicators

Use the Standards and Quality Indicators in Appendix 1 as the coaching program's standards of excellence.

» Which standards are the most helpful or relevant for your instructional coaching program evaluation?

» Have the standards you selected been clearly communicated to and discussed with all coaching stakeholders before evaluating them?

STEP 2: Compare the Standards and Quality Indicators to What Coaches Do

Examine the Quality Indicators for each Standard (Appendix 1) to see which elements of a particular success factor are most important to evaluate in your context.

» Which Quality Indicators are the most helpful or relevant for your instructional coaching program evaluation?

» Will other coaching tasks outside of the Quality Indicators be measured to determine program success? If so, create Quality Indicators for those tasks.

» Have all of the Quality Indicators you selected been clearly communicated to and discussed with all coaching stakeholders before evaluating them?

STEP 3: Determine Types of Data and Evidence That
Demonstrate Performance

*Determine how to measure the Quality Indicators you selected. The
following data pieces are most helpful in evaluating coaching success:*

» Number of PEERS goals that coaches have set and achieved
with teachers

» Number of Impact Cycles that coaches and teachers have
started and the number of cycles completed

» A time log demonstrating that coaches are spending the
majority of their time at school working in Impact Cycles with
teachers

» Feedback from teachers that attests to both the coaches'
partnership approach and to the implementation of the
Impact Cycle

» How will you measure each Quality Indicator you selected?

» Which types of evidence will be most helpful to track progress
for each?

» Have all of the data points and evidence pieces you selected
been clearly communicated to and discussed with all
coaching stakeholders before evaluating them?

STEP 4: Use Data to Make Judgments About Performance and to
Shape Goals for Improvement

*Examine our rubric for evaluating instructional coaching programs in
Appendix 7.*

» Which elements of the rubric will you use in your program
evaluation?

» How should you structure the evaluation to ensure that every
element is aligned with research and with best practices in
evaluation?

» How will you communicate the evaluation purpose and
process to all coaching stakeholders before evaluation begins?

» How will you use the data and feedback from the audit to
evaluate the future direction of the program?

» How will you ensure that you encourage the voices of all stakeholders in analyzing the data and feedback in making decisions about future directions for the program?

Make Final Decisions:

» How will you conduct any interviews or focus groups?
» How will you cull, calculate, and report the data?
» How will you communicate the audit results to all stakeholders?
» How will you ensure transparency throughout the audit process?
» How will you ensure that we use the data to improve the program?
» How will you continue to reflect on the decisions made and actions taken as a result of the audit?

WHAT WE LEARNED FROM THE AUDIT PROCESS

Although assisting Katy ISD in their evaluation goals was our main objective in the audit process, we also learned more about program evaluation during that process, and that knowledge now informs the writing of this book and our work with school districts. In some cases, the learning for us occurred during the audit with Katy ISD, but in many other cases, simply the process of working as an organization to develop materials and procedures with and for them spawned thinking about what might work best and pitfalls that may occur, regardless of whether Katy ISD experienced any of those pitfalls during the actual audit.

As districts go about planning their own evaluation processes, we suspect that they will also learn a great deal while planning the evaluation. Two aspects of our new learning were related to whether to use "insiders" or "outsiders" as evaluators and the importance of transparency in the process.

Insider versus outsider evaluators.

As part of the Katy ISD coaching audit, we at ICG knew going in that as evaluators who are not a part of the Katy ISD staff, we would have an obvious benefit: People outside of a school district tend to see subtleties of district operations and culture that people within that culture cannot see or cannot see clearly because they are emotionally attached to that culture and/or to the coaching program.

Because of that more objective perspective, outside auditors can shine light on issues that leaders had not known were influencing program success positively or negatively. Even with outside auditors, audits can confirm district perceptions about the program and the district as a whole. In other words, some results from an outside audit may show districts "what we already knew." That's a good thing. The audit ties data to perceptions that demonstrate their validity and can move those perceptions over to the category of "facts."

A significant disadvantage of using an outside organization to conduct an audit is that outside auditors need more time to learn about a district's internal structure, roles within the system, professional culture, and operational nuances. While providing that time results in better data analysis, clearer explanation of results, and more relevant and helpful ideas for how to improve, time is nevertheless a rare and valuable commodity.

Ann's past work with Katy ISD gave her an advantage in this area because she already knew a great deal about the district's coaching operations. Nonetheless, she and our other ICG staff members still needed time to confirm their understanding of the people, policies, and programs involved in coaching to ensure that the audit process would be accurate and helpful.

Specifically, ICG staff members worked with Katy ISD to examine which data would be most helpful, the best ways to collect those data, how to organize focus groups to encourage candor among participants, and how to ensure confidentiality across audit processes.

Audit Transparency.

To justify the time and effort of conducting a program audit, leaders all along the chain of command must fully support the process. In particular, they need to be

» willing to examine the audit data openly and discuss them realistically,

» willing to share the audit results with stakeholders with a high level of transparency, and

» committed to making changes based on the audit results.

When developing an audit process, evaluators must consider whether certain stakeholders are willing to act on the results in a meaningful way and, in that connection, what might be the best way of communicating data to them, especially if the data are not as positive as a particular stakeholder group may wish. Presenting data with sensitivity and in such a way that stakeholders can really "hear" them is important to motivate work toward improvement.

An instructional coaching audit process will undoubtedly surface coaching-specific concerns (e.g., coaches' concerns about role clarity, how coaches spend their work time, teacher resistance to coaching, level of Impact Cycle implementation), but district issues may arise as well, including budget and staffing priorities, hiring practices, leadership communication, and treatment of teachers in general.

For example, during an audit, leaders may discover that coaches spend significantly more time in quasi-administrative roles than they had realized. That discovery could result in new awareness about the need for more administrative positions in the school budget. Making that change can have a ripple effect on other programs and positions in the system, all of which may bring about new stresses and frustrations for everyone but could result in long-term positive change. To enter an audit process involves understanding that confronting such realities is a part of leadership and determining what is best for students and merely a hassle to be avoided. Such downstream complications can involve sensitive issues for all stakeholders, so leaders need to be prepared to discuss their own improvement in the process and not just that of coaches.

If, on the other hand, leaders are willing to acknowledge only certain issues raised by the audit or to make only small changes in response to the recommendations, then stakeholders may end up perceiving the audit process as a waste of time and resources. Instead, by approaching the audit realistically, with transparency, and with a willingness to make deep (and potentially difficult) change, leaders honor the voices of everyone who participated in the process and build trust across the district.

IMPORTANCE OF COMMUNICATION

Creating safe environments that encourage the voices of all stakeholders is just as important when evaluating programs as it is when evaluating instructional coaches. As we described in chapter 2, resources such as *Better Conversations* (Knight, 2016) and *The Leader's Guide to Coaching in Schools* (Campbell & van Nieuwerburgh (2018) are helpful for leaders who want to improve in creating those environments. One additional element of complexity that leaders must navigate at the program level involves an aspect of coaching that can muddy the communication waters: The coach as go-between.

Coaches tell us that, because they interact frequently with teachers, school administrators, and district administrators, they often operate as a sort of "go-between" in both school- and district-level communication. One coach we have worked with referred to these types of situations as "communication triangles."

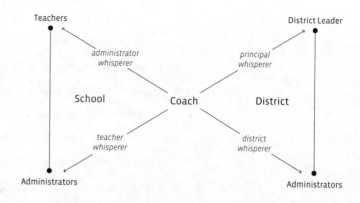

» **TRIANGLE 1:** At the school level, the coach serves as an "administrator whisperer" for teachers and as a "teacher whisperer" for administrators.
» **TRIANGLE 2:** At the district level, the coach serves as a "principal whisperer" for district leaders and as a "district whisperer" for administrators.

In other words, coaches find themselves interpreting (for lack of a better word) the policies, intentions, and/or attitudes of one group to another. Some of this dynamic is unavoidable. One advantage of coaching, in Sharon's experience, is that it gave her a deeper understanding of school- and district-level decisions because she wasn't solely viewing policy from the teacher perspective but had to view it from an implementation standpoint as well. With that understanding, she actively worked to bridge communication gaps among job roles.

But serving as an interpreter of sorts is exhausting and can create other communication problems for coaches. In a program evaluation conversation, for example, coaches may feel like they cannot be completely candid about their thoughts because they feel the pressure to interpret/advocate for teachers, school leaders, and/or district leaders at the same time. They may feel like honesty about a particular concern constitutes a betrayal of one of those groups of colleagues whom they value.

These communication triangles make providing coaches with a safe environment especially important. Coaches need to know that the boundaries of their teacher confidentiality policy will be respected when discussing the coaching program (i.e., that coaches will not be asked to name teachers and specific teachers' issues in the evaluation process), that they can voice ideas and concerns without negative repercussions, and that everyone in the evaluation process assumes the coaches' deep level of respect for all of the people in the school and district.

For all professionals (or, one could argue, all humans), communication should always be a focus area for improvement. How we talk about data, how we talk about performance, and how we talk about improvement all demonstrate our level of respect for our colleagues, our level of openness to new ideas, and the kind of professional culture we are creating. To build a strong program in which everyone feels engaged and hopeful for the future, leaders must create environments in which everyone feels safe to say what they think and know that their voices matter.

System Responsibility for Coach Success

WHY SYSTEM SUPPORT MATTERS

Because so much of coaching success depends on leaders, leaders bear as much (if not more) of the responsibility for coaching success as coaches do (Thomas, 2018b). System support can easily become an area that is dismissed in a coaching program evaluation. Evaluators may feel that, "Of course, we support coaches.

That's why we're doing this evaluation." But a concerted focus on the extent to which system support occurs is vital in determining the path forward for coaching. When system support is lacking in any of the areas we describe in this section, that lack will show up in terms of coaching results. If the school or district is not providing sound and consistent support, then, frankly, any failure of coaching to influence student data is not the coaches' fault.

For example, districts will sometimes say to us, "We love the Impact Cycle, and we want our coaches to do that work with teachers, but we need coaching to remain compulsory for teachers and not be a choice. Also, we don't think we can allow coaching interactions to be confidential. How can coaches get teachers to be less resistant in working deeply with them in that situation?" Coaches can't solve problems that leaders create. Only leaders can do that. Research clearly shows that a structure involving no choice or confidentiality is a barrier to teachers' engagement with coaches. To reduce that resistance, leaders need to change that structure, not believe that coaches can figure out some path around that problematic structure. Holding coaches responsible for teacher engagement is not fair in a situation like that, and leaders need to accept responsibility for that problem as part of evaluating coaching success.

In our experience, administrators can make or break coaching, and when they break it, it's typically unintentional—they just don't realize what kinds of support are necessary.

WHAT SYSTEM SUPPORT LOOKS LIKE

In his book *The Definitive Guide to Instructional Coaching* (Knight, 2022), Jim reinforces the importance of intentional focus on these nine key areas:

1. **UNDERSTAND CHANGE:** School and district leaders need a shared understanding about the research on adults and change

and why a partnership approach is more effective in bringing about change than a traditional top-down approach to coaching.

2.   **HIRE EFFECTIVE COACHES:** School and district leaders should focus on the most important aspects of the coaching role itself when hiring new coaches instead of automatiucally hiring people perceived as the "best" teachers (see chapter 4).

3.   **ESTABLISH DISTRICT-WIDE UNDERSTANDING OF COACHING:** School and district leaders need to ensure that they have multiple opportunities to communicate with staff about what coaching is and isn't in order to help coaches build trust and relationships that will lead to deep Impact Cycle work.

4.   **ENSURE THEORETICAL ALIGNMENT:** School and district leaders need to understand the difference between "surface" and "deep coaching" (see chapter 2) to ensure that teachers hear a consistent message about what the coach role entails.

5.   **CLARIFY ROLES AND TIME:** School and district leaders need to continually address the issue of role clarity so that coaches engage in research-based coaching practices for most of their work time. School and district leaders need to ensure that coaches' work time is protected for those research-based tasks, despite competing priorities.

6.   **ADDRESS CONFIDENTIALITY:** School and district leaders need to ensure that a clear coaching confidentiality policy is in place so that teachers feel safe in working with coaches.

7.   **CREATE A LEARNING CULTURE:** Leaders need to create a psychologically safe environment in the school. Amy Edmondson (2019) stresses the importance of work environments in which employees feel both accountable to high standards of performance and also safe to take risks. She calls this "The Learning Zone." Administrators need to foster a school culture that operates as a Learning Zone so

that teachers feel safe to engage in coaching and coaches feel safe to flexibly support different teachers in different ways. Administrators should also "walk the talk" of partnership and coaching as much as possible. From using the Partnership Principles as often as feasible in daily interactions to using video for leaders' own professional growth to asking for coaching support for themselves, administrators who walk the talk create school cultures that support coaching and that focus on growth for everyone.

8.   **BUILD LEARNING ARCHITECTURE:** School and district leaders need to map out a "learning architecture" to ensure that the best possible professional learning is in place for everyone in any role, including coaches. How professionals learn, what they learn, and the environemnts they learn should all be a part of that learning architecture to ensure that everyone is learning and growing. Coaches are often neglected as learners in schools because they deliver so much of the professional learning, so school and district leaders need to ensure that coaches have the time and ability to continue their own professional learning as much as anyone in the building.

9.   **ENSURE LEADERSHIP SUPPORT:** School and district leaders need to be willing to "run interference" for them with people both in their schools and at the district level on all of the above issues. Coaches need leaders who are willing to do that on the coaches' behalf to ensure role clarity, time for what is most important for students, and confidentiality for teachers. Coaches also need encouragement and support as much as any other employee, and meeting weekly or every other week enables both the coach and the administrator to talk about issues affecting the school and coaching, gives the administrator time for the ongoing feedback that we described in chapter 2, and ensures that the coach has regular, ongoing, safe support.

Coaches are partly responsible for coaching success, and so are administrators. Leaders who are open to data on how they're doing in supporting coaching are likely to improve their coaching program and the extent to which coaching positively influences student data.

⊔⊔⊔

School leaders deal with difficult realities every day. No one ever has enough people in any school building to do all of the jobs necessary to serve students fully and best. Programs—even really good programs—are not sustainable unless leaders provide consistent support for those programs. Part of that support involves program evaluation. One of the best ways to ensure coaching success is to have a plan in place for

1.   knowing what the district wants the coaching program to be and do (what we call the Standards and Quality Indicators [Appendix 1]),

2.   developing a system for evaluating the program against those Standards, and

3.   determining a process by which improvement happens based on the evaluation data.

Such a plan not only helps ensure that coaching has a deeper and broader impact across classrooms and schools; it also ensures that leaders can defend the need for the program with accurate information about its success.

Developing and carrying out thoughtful evaluation programs take time, money, and energy, but they are important in keeping valuable coaching resources available for teachers and in making the impact of coaching on students as significant as it can be.

 ## To Sum Up

---

» To evaluate coaching programs, leaders need to use the Seven Success Factors to guide program evaluation, conduct regular instructional coaching program audits, and focus on communication skills in evaluation conversations.

» For coaching programs to be most effective, leaders must embrace their role in program success. They must include system support measures as part of any program evaluation and consider the areas where they can improve to help coaches improve.

Making It Real

To make effective coaching program evaluation real, examine the Standards and Quality Indicators (Appendix 1) in relation to your coaching program. Are those Standards an accurate description of how coaching works in your school or district? Next, examine the rubric for evaluating coaching programs in Appendix 7. Would that rubric aid in determining areas for growth for your program? Once the evaluation team is clear on what it is measuring and how the team is measuring it, the team can then reflect on the description of the coaching program audit in this chapter and determine whether that process is a good one for your purposes or whether you would want to make modifications. After such reflection, the team should have a good handle on where to start to make the evaluation process a reality.

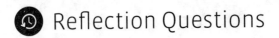 # Reflection Questions

What was most valuable part of this chapter?

....

....

....

....

....

....

Which elements of research-based instructional coaching are already evident in your coaching program?

....

....

....

....

....

Which elements of research-based coaching would you like to add to your evaluation system?

....

....

....

....

....

Would the teacher, coach, and administrator forms from chapter 2 be helpful in aligning your program evaluation process with research-based coaching? What would you modify or add to them?

....

....

....

....

....

....

Which types of data or evidence would you want to see as part of
the program's evaluation process?

....

....

....

....

....

....

What communication issues do you need to be aware of or work
on as part of the program evaluation process?

....

....

....

....

....

....

Going Deeper

Evaluating program success in any profession is complex. We recommend several resources to help you go deeper on program evaluation for your coaches. In *Kirkpatrick's Four Levels of Training Evaluation,* James and Wendy Kirkpatrick (2016) examine the importance of focusing on the four levels of results, behavior, learning, and reaction in determining a program's next steps. They also dive deeply into data and how to use data in program evaluation, and they provide several real-world case studies that demonstrate application of their protocol.

Specific to coaching in schools, Joellen Killion, Chris Bryan, and Heather Clifton (2020) examine the issue of coach evaluation in chapter 10 of the second edition of their book, *Coaching Matters.* In addition, Killion's 2018 book, *Assessing Impact,* provides readers with an examination of how to best evaluate professional learning of all types, not strictly coaching. A deeper understanding of evaluation in general helps leaders to distinguish among the best evaluation practices for the various types of professional learning experiences in their schools. That clarity helps to improve professional growth for everyone.

CHAPTER 4

RECRUITING AND HIRING INSTRUCTIONAL COACHES

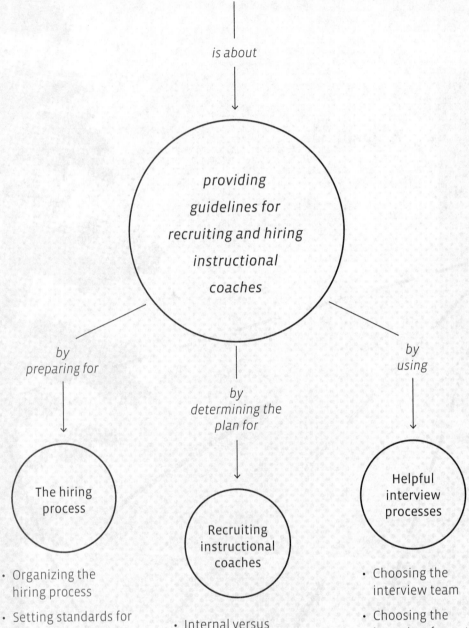

is about

providing guidelines for recruiting and hiring instructional coaches

by preparing for

by determining the plan for

by using

The hiring process

Recruiting instructional coaches

Helpful interview processes

- Organizing the hiring process

- Setting standards for the job description and the hiring decision

- Internal versus external recruitment

- Passive job seekers versus active job seekers

- Managing the candidate experience

- Choosing the interview team

- Choosing the interview format

- Choosing the interview questions

CHAPTER

04

RECRUITING AND HIRING

INSTRUCTIONAL COACHES

 SNAPSHOT:

This chapter presents processes for recruiting and

hiring instructional coaches that support both best

coaching practices and best hiring practices. If you

are not part of the coach recruitment or hiring

process in your district, you can move on to chapter

5 to learn ways to strengthen coaching to ensure its

lasting impact on schools.

From the time she was a young child, Letitia was a helper. Whether assisting her mother with yardwork, acting as a safety patrol in the fifth grade, or volunteering with Habitat for Humanity with the Student Council in high school, Letitia relished service.

That characteristic led her to become an elementary school teacher, a role in which she enjoyed every aspect of the job. Working with students, planning lessons, attending school spirit days, participating in professional development sessions in which she learned new skills and strategies—she loved it all. She still had much to learn to improve her skills as a teacher, but she knew she was making a difference with her students, particularly in establishing a safe, respectful, and loving classroom environment.

Early in her teaching years, Letitia became intrigued by a job she had not known existed: school instructional coach. That role appealed to her deep need to make a difference in the lives of students. "If I support teachers, then I can make an even bigger difference in the school system." After four years in the classroom, Letitia applied to become an instructional coach.

Across town, in a different elementary school, Lucas was mulling over the same job change. From his first year of teaching, Lucas had dazzled his administrators with his teaching ability, and he was quickly considered one of the top teachers in the district. Now, after teaching for 15 years, he was often approached about becoming an administrator, but he knew that role wasn't for him. He liked the idea of serving as an instructional coach, though. "For years, principals have been telling me that we need more teachers like me. Maybe that's what I should do—become a coach so that I can help more teachers be like me." In the end, he applied for the same job as Letitia.

Both Letitia and Lucas aced the screening interview. They were capable, qualified professionals, and Porter, a curriculum director who serves as the coaches' hiring manager, sensed no "red flags" about either of them. During the skills interview, Letitia demonstrated the ability to read people and situations and to empathize with their troubles, but her relatively short time as a teacher had her struggling on some issues regarding pedagogy and options for instructional strategies. Lucas, on the other hand, excelled on the questions involving knowledge of instructional strategies but was not as strong in demonstrating his ability to listen deeply and to engage as a partner with teachers. His responses to teacher concerns in the various coaching scenarios presented during the interview were to recommend strategies that had been successful in his own classroom. He vocalized that those tools should work just as well for anyone else's students as they had for his.

Letitia and Lucas both made it to the final interview, the model interview, in which they were to demonstrate their coaching skills in action. Letitia showed a deep respect for the teacher in her interview, a willingness to listen, and an understanding that she didn't have all of the answers but was open to finding various options that might help the teacher with his concern about his students. Lucas again relied on his own teaching experience to inform his suggestions regarding the teacher's concerns and sought to guide the teacher to his way of thinking about how to improve student achievement.

By the end of the interviews, Porter and the interview panel were torn: Lucas had such strong classroom experience and stellar recommendations, but Letitia outperformed him on coaching skills. Who will make the best coach?

The hiring process for instructional coaches is another area in which school and system administrators have a great deal of power to communicate coaching best practices and to ensure the success of the coaches and the coaching program. That said, the hiring process can also be subject to the same misconceptions as the other aspects of instructional coaching we've explored in this book, particularly the issue of which characteristics are most important in a new coach. For many hiring managers, as in the above scenario, Lucas would obviously be the best candidate. After examining the research on instructional coaching, however, Letitia emerges as quite the contender. This chapter explains why.

So far, we have explored how to evaluate instructional coaching and coaching programs because evaluation is an area of concern we hear worldwide. A related issue involves the best ways to recruit and hire coaches to ensure that the people who support teachers are the best possible educators to fill those roles. As Jim says, "The most important factor in an instructional coaching program is having the right people in the coaching roles. Effective coaches impact not only teacher practice and student learning, but move the system in positive ways that can have an immeasurable impact on the system and culture" (Knight, 2022).

By now, readers likely will not be surprised to learn that role clarity is as important an issue when recruiting and hiring coaches as it is when evaluating them. Because hiring decisions involve processes and personnel district wide, the consequences—positive and negative—for how sound those hiring practices are will be widespread. Perceptions about the purpose of instructional coaching are embedded in the district's culture and policies. To ensure that the right people are in the right roles and that the roles are clear entails ensuring that all district functions support coaching best practices.

Recruiting and hiring instructional coaches doesn't just mean being clear about the coaching role; rather, hiring practices in general also involve legal concerns and best-practice issues. Because those practices are ever changing to meet the demands of the modern workplace, understanding their nuances is important for creating a successful hiring process.

Cappelli (2019) explains how the hiring practices of most organizations have changed over the last century.

> For most of the post–World War II era, large corporations went about hiring this way: Human resources experts prepared a detailed job analysis to determine what tasks the job required and what attributes a good candidate should have. Next, they did a job evaluation to determine how the job fit into the organizational chart and how much it should pay, especially compared with other jobs. Ads were posted, and applicants applied. Then came the task of sorting through the applicants. That included skills tests, reference checks, maybe personality and IQ tests, and extensive interviews to learn more about them as people. (p. 1)

Today, Cappelli (2019) asserts, hiring practices look different. "The majority of people who took a new job last year weren't searching for one: Somebody came and got them. Companies seek to fill their recruiting funnel with as many candidates as possible, especially 'passive candidates,' who aren't looking to move" (Cappelli, 2019, p. 1). Further, employers often "advertise jobs that don't exist, hoping to find people who might be useful later on or in a different context" (Cappelli, 2019, p. 1). Technology aids this approach, with apps and websites like LinkedIn, Indeed.com, and others enabling employers to seek out candidates themselves instead of waiting for candidates to come to them.

But even with these new approaches to creating a candidate pool, one key focus of hiring remains: How can we ensure that we get the best people in the right jobs? To do achieve that goal, employers must take active steps to ensure that all elements of their hiring process (from planning to hire, to recruitment, to the interview process, to the hiring decision) focus on the most important facets of that job. Cappelli (2019) says, "It's impossible to get better at hiring if you can't tell whether the candidates you select become good employees. If you don't know where you're going, any road will take you there. You must have a way to measure which employees are the best ones" (p. 7). The success of coaches and coaching programs begins by aligning the hiring process to the same standards and job expectations that we described as part of evaluation in chapters 2 and 3.

The Hiring Process

_____

The hiring process for a position in any organization involves more people than just the hiring manager and the selected candidate. Because of the legal and budgetary issues involved in hiring personnel, the human resources (HR) department typically works with hiring managers and other leaders to determine how, when, and whom to hire. In some cases, the school district's HR team may have a standard process that hiring managers must follow, but in other situations, depending on the job to be filled, hiring managers may have some flexibility. In this section, we describe the important components of the hiring process for instructional coaches to ensure that the process is aligned with best practices in both hiring and instructional coaching.

ORGANIZING THE HIRING PROCESS

The more time the hiring manager invests in organizing the hiring process, the clearer the job description will be, the better the candidate pool will be, the more informative the interview process will be, and the clearer the hiring decision will be.

THE IMPORTANCE OF HUMAN RESOURCES

The HR professionals in a school district are valuable partners when hiring instructional coaches. They know how to navigate the complexities of laws surrounding hiring employees, and, although their role may vary in some ways from district to district, they generally support hiring managers in several areas related to logistics and the law. HR departments often

» review and provide feedback on interview questions,

» review and provide feedback on hiring processes (if hiring managers do not have to follow an already established process),

» provide support in recruiting candidates through job postings and marketing,

» conduct any required background checks or drug testing on external candidates,

» make the job offer to the selected candidate on behalf of the district,

» field salary and benefits questions from candidates, and

» inform the other candidates that they didn't get the job.

Approaching HR professionals as partners throughout the hiring process can ensure that hiring managers are following the law, providing prospective candidates with clarity about the job and the hiring process, and casting a wide net to engage as many qualified candidates as possible.

SOUND HIRING PROCESSES

Noe and associates (2008) recommend the following standards for employers to use when determining the processes they will use to hire employees.

» **RELIABILITY:** "the consistency of a performance measure" (p. 227). To hire instructional coaches, employers must ask, "Does the hiring process focus on a specific set of standards for coaches that can be reliably scored by multiple evaluators?"

» **VALIDITY:** "The extent to which a performance measure assesses all the relevant—and only the relevant—aspects of job performance" (p. 231). To hire instructional coaches, employers must ask, "Does the hiring process focus only on the most relevant aspects of research-based instructional coaching and the other specific tasks we expect coaches to do?"

» **GENERALIZABILITY:** "The degree to which the validity of a selection method established in one context extends to other contexts" (p. 235). To hire instructional coaches, employers must ask, "Does the hiring process provide standards and methods for choosing instructional coaches who will likely be successful in any school across the district?"

» **UTILITY:** "The degree to which the information provided by selection methods enhances the effectiveness of selecting personnel in real organizations" (p. 236). To hire instructional coaches, employers must ask, "Has the hiring process resulted in choosing people who have been successful in the coaching role?"

» **LEGALITY:** "All selection methods should conform to existing laws and existing legal precedents" (p. 237). To hire instructional coaches, employers must ask, "Does the hiring process follow all federal and state laws regarding the recruitment and hiring of employees?"

To guide schools and districts in recruiting and hiring coaches, we frame this section around a checklist that can help hiring managers to create humanizing hiring experiences that involve choosing the best people for the role.

 ## PLANNING FOR RECRUITING AND HIRING COACHES CHECKLIST

PLANNING FOR RECRUITING AND HIRING COACHES	✓
Contact Human Resources to determine existing policy regarding recruitment and hiring practices and to establish a partnership with them in the process.	○
Determine the job standards for the instructional coach role (use Appendices 1 and 2 as resources).	○
Create the job description around the selected standards.	○
Determine the best evidence pieces to use in using the rubric to score candidates and create a scoring tool for each element of the job description (use Appendix 8 as a resource).	○
Select the interview panel.	○
With the panel and HR, develop questions for the screening interview, skills interview, and model interview.	○
Advertise the position as appropriate.	○
Conduct the screening interviews, skills interviews, and model interviews.	○

Analyze the data from all of the evidence pieces.	○
Make the hiring decision.	○
Communicate the hiring decision to all candidates.	○

The first part of determining the process for hiring is clarity around the standards for the position. Having clear standards ensures that critical documents like the job description and application communicate the role effectively and allows the hiring team to set scoring parameters around the most relevant aspects of the job.

SETTING STANDARDS FOR THE JOB DESCRIPTION AND THE HIRING DECISION

Often, we see districts begin to hire instructional coaches without a clear vision of what they want coaches to do. Districts accurately identify a need for deeper and more consistent teacher support, but then they assume that if they hire great teachers to fill those coaching roles, those coaches will automatically know what to do to support adults. But as we describe in chapter 2, that's just not the case. Supporting adults in learning new teaching practices is not the same as supporting children in learning new academic content. In fact, when coaches default to approaching adults in the same ways they approached children, teachers are much less willing to work with them.

The lack of clarity about what coaches do begins with the job description. Candidates for any job want to know, "Exactly what would I be signing up for? What exactly do I have to do?" Coach job descriptions often provide little help in answering those questions. This lack of clarity can cause big problems after the coach is hired. If coaches don't know what success is, and if administrators aren't clear about what coaches can and cannot do, problems are sure to arise (as we describe in chapters 2 and 3). Clarity up front benefits everyone.

For us to create one standard job descrption for instructional coaches for this book is likely not helpful. We recommend that instructional coaching be grounded in partnership always but involve deep, Impact Cycle coaching for approximately 60-70% of the coach's work time to ensure an impact on student growth. That means that 30-40% of the coach's time will involve other responsibilities such as implementation support, personal knowledge building, or other forms of "surface" coaching (see chapter 2). Using the tools we suggest below, districts may find creating the job description themselves to be a process that

» involves their team's own deep thinking in determining the parameters of the coaching role to ensure good communication about and support for the role,
» focuses on achieving that target in Impact Cycle work of 60-70%, and
» best meets the needs of the school when determining how coaches should spend their non-Impact Cycle time.

When developing the job description for an instructional coach and the corresponding scoring system for hiring one, we recommend using the same tools that we created for evaluating coaches in chapter 2.

USING EVALUATION TOOLS TO DEVELOP THE JOB DESCRIPTION

Appendix 1 delineates the Standards and Quality Indicators for instructional coaches and should be the foundation of any instructional coach's job description. By focusing on the most student-focused elements of coaching, candidates will have a clearer sense of what the role is and what it isn't. In addition, the job description can then be another way to foster a consistent view of what coaching is in the district.

The hiring manager and HR should develop a list of duties, skills, and responsibilities based on the Standards, and that also includes any other elements of the coaching role beyond the standards. Some of our partner school districts from California, Illinois, Michigan, Texas, and Virginia shared their coach job descriptions with us. The box below shows a sample of the Impact Cycle-related and non-Impact Cycle-related items they include.

SAMPLE ITEMS FOR INSTRUCTIONAL COACH JOB DESCRIPTIONS

IMPACT CYCLE-RELATED

Instructional coaches

» Exhibit a high level of ethics and confidentiality in regard to student and teacher records and classroom performance.

» Collaborate with colleagues within and across content areas, grade levels, and other instructional coaches.

» Guide and assist teachers in selecting strategies, resources, and materials that promote student engagement, learning, and problem solving based on different learning preferences and readiness levels.

» Increase the quality and effectiveness of classroom instruction through collaborating, co-planning, coaching cycle completion, fostering trusting relationships with staff, and supporting the learning process.

» Share with campus staff research, best practices, resources, instructional technology tools, and/or emerging trends aligned with district curriculum and beliefs.

» Assist teachers in developing a comprehensive understanding of subject content and curriculum standards.

» Demonstrate knowledge of best practices.

» Develop teachers' capacity to meet the needs of diverse student populations.

» Build teachers' capacity to utilize a variety of data to make informed decisions about instructional practices and high-impact strategies.

» Facilitate conversations using data to drive instructional decisions.

» Support implementation of effective instructional strategies.

» Engage teachers in reflective thinking while looking at their own instructional practices critically and analytically.

NON-IMPACT CYCLE-RELATED

Instructional coaches

» Support teachers' development by co-teaching, modeling, observing, and providing feedback.

» Assist district and campus administration in identifying programmatic growth areas for both the campus and grade-level teams.

» Serve as the lead learners through modeling and facilitating learning opportunities for campus staff.

» Work with teachers to align instruction with state standards.

» Facilitate inter-visitations for teachers to see and learn from other classrooms.

» Organize and facilitate study groups, on site workshops, and book studies.

» Work with collaborative groups to examine student work and plan instruction.

» Read and share research with staff.

» Attend coaching trainings and bring information and strategies back to building staff.

» Help to establish common vocabulary, background knowledge and experiences, and collaborative relationships.

Some districts also specify what coaching is *not* in their job descriptions for coaches. For example, Rantoul (IL) Township High School specifies that

"The role of the coach does not include:

» Evaluating teachers

» Providing information that would be used for evaluation

» Serving as a substitute teacher

» Serving as the principal designee

» Performing clerical duties outside the primary job performance criteria

» Disciplining students in an administrative capacity"

Clarity on exactly what the job is *and is not* helps potential candidates a great deal when deciding whether to apply for the job, and it makes interview situations and hiring decisions much clearer and easier for everyone involved.

One element of the job description that may not seem important (particularly when hiring within the district) is to be sure to include salary information on the job description. Aretha Young, an HR professional in Maryland, encourages salary clarity for coaches because prospective candidates ask for clarity around that issue all the time. The coach role is a "lateral" move for teachers in most districts, but many still want confirmation that their salary would not change. From a coaching perspective, salary clarity makes sense, too. It reinforces the fact that serving as a coach is not a "promotion"; it's a partnership between peers.

To aid schools and school districts in gaining clarity about what coaches do, in his latest book (Knight, 2022), Jim created a one-page "scorecard" that can inform the instructional coach job description. Districts can develop their own scorecards before getting down to the specifics of a job description to ensure that the "big picture" concerns of what coaching is and what coaches do are clear to everyone in the hiring process before communicating the role to candidates.

INSTRUCTIONAL COACH ONE-PAGE SUMMARY

MISSION

To partner with teachers so that teachers move through coaching cycles that involve getting a clear picture of reality, setting PEERS goals, identifying, explaining, and modeling strategies, and partnering with teachers to make adaptations until goals are set.

OUTCOMES

» Within the first 60 days on the job, the instructional coach will be proficient in using the Impact Cycle (described in Chapters 2-5 of The Impact Cycle and summarized by the checklist on p.107 in The Impact Cycle Reflection Guide).

» Within the first 60 days, the instructional coach will be proficient in describing and modeling the teaching strategies included in the district's Instructional Playbook.

» Within the first 60 days, the instructional coach will be proficient in gathering and explaining the various types of engagement and achievement data described in *The Definitive Guide to Instructional Coaching*.

» By the end of the academic year, the instructional coach will have partnered with at least 40 teachers to set and meet PEERS goals.

» Each week the instructional coach will watch at least one video of his/her coaching conversations and apply the after-action review questions ("What was supposed to happen?," "What really happened?," "What accounts for the difference?," "What will I do next time?) to identify areas for improvement.

COMPETENCIES.

The instructional coach is:

» A learner: open to change, seeking out new information, flexible and adaptive in her/his implementation of materials, seeking out and internalizing feedback until proficient in strategies, coachable.

» An excellent communicator: demonstrating outstanding listening and questioning skills, and able to make positive emotional connections with others

» An encourager: positive, affirmative, nonjudgmental, fully present in conversation, and respectful of teachers and all other educators and students.

» Reliable: organized and keen to provide scaffolding for others who are not highly organized persistent, ambitious to change.

Source: Jim Knight,
The Definitive Guide to
Instructional Coaching, 2022.

Once the standards and job description are clear, the hiring manager must decide on the types of evidence that candidates must provide to show their qualifications. Noe and associates (2008) describe seven types of data that employers most commonly use when making hiring decisions.

1. Interviews
2. References, biographical data, and application information
3. Physical ability tests
4. Cognitive ability tests
5. Personal inventories
6. Work samples
7. Honesty tests and drug tests

In our experience, use of those types of data varies greatly when hiring instructional coaches. The ones we see most often take shape in the following ways.

Interviews.

Interviews are common practice when hiring instructional coaches, but, as Noe and associates (2008) explain, "Unfortunately, the long history of research on the employment interview suggests that, without proper care, it can be unreliable, low in validity, and biased against a number of different groups" (p. 241). To increase the validity of interviews, Noe and associates (2008) recommend

» asking relevant questions,

» asking every candidate the same questions,

» using a ratings system for interviews that is based on observable items,

» using a structured note-taking system that helps to justify ratings,

» using situational questions to help predict job performance,

» using multiple interviewers trained in the area of bias,

» video recording the interview and sharing it with others involved in the process (versus sending the candidate around to be interviewed multiple times), and

» approaching candidates as "witnesses of facts" and not "judges." (p. 243)

(We examine interview questions and procedure later in this chapter.)

References, biographical data, and application information.
Employers can best verify the information they glean from interviews by hearing the reports of the candidate's references. Noe and associates (2008) caution that letters of reference are not very helpful because the candidate picks the letter writer, and the information the employer receives is limited to whatever the letter writer decided to include. More helpful are actual conversations with the person providing the reference as a way to confirm the perceptions formed by information from the interviews and from any application materials the candidate submitted.

Physical ability tests.
Instructional coach candidates will not likely need to prove that they can lift 40 lbs. to become coaches, for example, but they may need to demonstrate the ability to travel to multiple schools during the workday, to be in particular locations at specific times, and/or to work beyond the standard duty-day hours as part of the coaching role.

Cognitive ability tests.

Noe and associates (2008) describe these types of tests in relation to standardized intelligence assessments, something that is not likely to be a part of hiring instructional coaches. For coaching positions, testing a candidate's "thinking" will more likely involve responses to scenarios in behavioral or situational questions during skills interviews and model interviews (which we describe later in this chapter). In those circumstances, employers would likely give more weight to the candidate's level of emotional intelligence than to the candidate's perceived intellectual prowess.

Work samples.

Candidates for instructional coaching positions may bring to the interviews portfolios containing artifacts of their accomplishments in teaching and/or in leading or participating in professional development (PD) activities. Additionally, candidates may share video recordings of themselves coaching or delivering PD to adults. Some interview processes may involve role-playing scenarios that serve as a form of "audition" as well. All of these materials have benefits in showing the candidate's history and skills in supporting other adults in learning and change as well as their commitment to professional learning.

Hiring managers will need to compare one candidate's evidence pieces with others. To do so means having a clear rubric that makes scoring each candidate as simple and accurate as possible.

USING EVALUATION TOOLS IN THE HIRING DECISION

Appendix 2 contains the rubric for evaluating instructional coaches, and several sections of it can be modified for use in scoring candidates in the hiring process. Expecting candidates to have a deep knowledge of the elements of the Impact Cycle is likely not fair, but scoring the candidate's interviews and written materials using the Partnership Principles (Figure 4.1), Communication Habits and Skills (Figure 4.2), and Leadership (Figure 4.3) sections of the rubric could be useful to the hiring team.

Figure 4.1:
_____

STANDARD 1

PARTNERSHIP PRINCIPLES

No matter how much knowledge instructional coaches have, they will not be effective change leaders unless they understand the complexities of helping and working with adults. Instructional coaches demonstrate that they understand how to interact with adults in ways that do not engender resistance.

QUALITY INDICATOR 1.1

The coach uses a dialogical approach (Knight, 2017) to coaching, in which the coach and teachers are partners who use their collective strengths to make powerful classroom changes for students.

QUALITY INDICATOR 1.2

The coach consistently embodies the Partnership Principles (Knight, 2011) in coaching interactions to build trusting relationships with teachers and school and system leaders.

SCORE OF 1	SCORE OF 2	SCORE OF 3	SCORE OF 4
the coach does not work with teachers as a partner	the coach unevenly works with teachers as a partner	the coach consistently works with teachers as a partner	the coach extensively works with teachers as a partner
the coach minimally uses a dialogical approach to coaching (Equality, Choice, Voice, and Reflection and Demonstrating Empathy, Listening, and Asking Better Questions)	the coach inconsistently uses a dialogical approach to coaching (Equality, Choice, Voice, and Reflection and Demonstrating Empathy, Listening, and Asking Better Questions)	the coach often uses a dialogical approach to coaching (Equality, Choice, Voice, and Reflection and Demonstrating Empathy, Listening, and Asking Better Questions)	the coach extensively uses a dialogical approach to coaching (Equality, Choice, Voice, and Reflection and Demonstrating Empathy, Listening, and Asking Better Questions)
the coach does not share expertise with the teacher positioned as the decision-maker	the coach inconsistently shares expertise with the teacher positioned as the decision-maker	the coach often shares expertise with the teacher positioned as the decision-maker	the coach effectively shares expertise with the teacher positioned as the decision-maker
the coach does not work with school and/or district leadership to clarify the theoretical basis of dialogical coaching so that the coach and leaders agree on what "instructional coaching" is	the coach infrequently works with school and/or district leadership to clarify the theoretical basis of dialogical coaching so that the coach and leaders agree on what "instructional coaching" is	the coach consistently works with school and/or district leadership to clarify the theoretical basis of dialogical coaching so that the coach and leaders agree on what "instructional coaching" is	the coach extensively works with school and/or district leadership to clarify the theoretical basis of dialogical coaching so that the coach and leaders agree on what "instructional coaching" is

STANDARD 5

COMMUNICATION HABITS AND SKILLS

Because coaching involves communication, instructional coaches continually engage in improving their communication skills and in communicating about coaching with all school stakeholders to build a collaborative school culture.

QUALITY INDICATOR 5.1

The coach communicates with teachers in a spirit of partnership as evidenced by the use of the *Better Conversations* Habits (Demonstrating Empathy, Listening, Fostering Dialogue, Asking Better Questions, Making Emotional Connections, Being a Witness to the Good, Finding Common Ground, Controlling Toxic Emotions, Redirecting Toxic Conversations, and Building Trust) as appropriate in coaching conversations (Knight, 2016).

QUALITY INDICATOR 5.2

The coach communicates about the coaching role, the coaching approach, and the coaching process regularly with school and system administrators and teachers to foster a collaborative school culture.

	SCORE OF 1	SCORE OF 2	SCORE OF 3	SCORE OF 4
COACHING APPROACH				
	the coach does not a dialogical approach to coaching (Equality, Choice, Voice, and Reflection and Demonstrating Empathy, Listening, and Asking Better Questions)	the coach inconsistently uses a dialogical approach to coaching (Equality, Choice, Voice, and Reflection and Demonstrating Empathy, Listening, and Asking Better Questions)	the coach often uses a dialogical approach to coaching (Equality, Choice, Voice, and Reflection and Demonstrating Empathy, Listening, and Asking Better Questions)	the coach extensively uses a dialogical approach to coaching (Equality, Choice, Voice, and Reflection and Demonstrating Empathy, Listening, and Asking Better Questions)
	the coach does not share expertise with the teacher positioned as the decision-maker	the coach minimally shares expertise with the teacher positioned as the decision-maker	the coach consistently shares expertise with the teacher positioned as the decision-maker	the coach effectively shares expertise with the teacher and clearly positions the teacher as the decision-maker
COMMUNICATION				
	the coach does not communicate about the coaching role with school and system administrators and teachers	the coach minimally communicates about the coaching role with school and system administrators and teachers	the coach consistently communicates about the coaching role regularly with school and system administrators and teachers	the coach extensively communicates about the coaching role regularly with school and system administrators and teachers
	the coach does not communicate about the coaching approach with school and system administrators and teachers	the coach minimally communicates about the coaching approach with school and system administrators and teachers	the coach consistently communicates about the coaching approach regularly with school and system administrators and teachers	the coach extensively communicates about the coaching approach regularly with school and system administrators and teachers
	the coach does not communicate about the coaching process with school and system administrators and teachers	the coach minimally communicates about the coaching process with school and system administrators and teachers	the coach consistently communicates about the coaching process regularly with school and system administrators and teachers	the coach extensively communicates about the coaching process regularly with school and system administrators and teachers
	the coach does not help foster a collaborative school culture	the coach minimally fosters a collaborative school culture	the coach consistently fosters a collaborative school culture	the coach significantly fosters a collaborative school culture

STANDARD 6

LEADERSHIP

Instructional coaches are emotionally intelligent, responsive to teachers, embody a stewardship approach during coaching, are ambitious for students, organized, and reliable (see Knight, 2016, chapter 9). In other words, effective coaches are effective leaders.

QUALITY INDICATOR 6.1

The coach has built trusting relationships with teachers that have resulted in many teachers choosing to work with the coach in Impact Cycles.

QUALITY INDICATOR 6.2

The coach has an exceptional level of instructional expertise and shares that knowledge with teachers as appropriate but does so dialogically as a partner, not as an "expert" or as an evaluator.

SCORE OF 1	SCORE OF 2	SCORE OF 3	SCORE OF 4
few teachers and/or an inconsistent number of teachers voluntarily choose to work with the coach	a small but consistent number teachers voluntarily choose to work with the coach	an appropriate and growing number of teachers voluntarily choose to work with the coach	a significant and growing number of teachers voluntarily choose to work with the coach
the coach does not interact with teachers and leaders as a partner	the coach inconsistently interacts with teachers and leaders as a partner and not as an "expert"	the coach consistently interacts with teachers and leaders as a partner and not as an "expert"	the coach extensively interacts with teachers and leaders as a partner and not as an "expert"

If the hiring decision involves more people than the hiring manager, then having that team meet to discuss scoring is an important part of the planning process. Discussing the standards, the rubric, and each type of evidence aids in ensuring consistency and the validity of the hiring process itself. Once the hiring process, standards, job description, evidence pieces, and rubric are fleshed out, then recruiting candidates can begin.

Recruiting Instructional Coaches

When hiring instructional coaches, just as the perception persists that "The best teachers make the best school administrators," leaders have a tendency to think that "the best teachers will make the best coaches." But the research on effective instructional coaches disagrees. "Though a prospective coach's resume may indicate experience and success as a classroom teacher, this does not necessarily signify a teacher's readiness for a staff development position" (Richard, 2003, as cited in Knight et al., 2010, p. 3).

In Knight et al.'s study (2010), one coaching coordinator explained that even "the best teacher in the world is not always going to be the best coach, because the best teacher doesn't always feel comfortable working with adults" (p. 7). Fernández-Aráoz, senior advisor at global executive search firm Egon Zehnder, sees this distinction in fields outside of education as well: "People are hired because of their academic achievement and experience, but fired for their emotional intelligence" (as cited in Knight, 2021, p. 1).

Knight et al. (2010) found that the most effective coaches

» embody an array of interpersonal skills that enable them to develop collaborative, professional relationships with teachers,

» effectively listen to the perspectives, opinions, and concerns of teachers,

» are learners who have a lot of useful knowledge and skills, and

» love their work, are skilled at creating coaching opportunities, while helping to build a cohesive school community.

Similarly, Rebecca Frazier's (2021) comprehensive study of the characteristics of effective coaches found that effective coaches are

» collaborative,

» caring,

» competent,

» authentic,

» quality communicators,

» inspirational,

» flexible,

» trustworthy,

» well-organized, and

» effective at modeling practices.

In summary, the results from these two studies, and our work in the field, show the importance of the coach's emotional intelligence (Knight, 2022).

INTERNAL VERSUS EXTERNAL RECRUITMENT

For most organizations, discussions about hiring "internally" or "externally" focus on whether to search for candidates from within the organization or outside of the organization, or both. School districts with multiple buildings have an added "internal versus external" layer when hiring coaches: whether to hire the coach for a specific school from within that school or to hire someone from another school building within the district to fill the role. These options are important to examine when planning for the hiring process.

INTERNAL VERSUS EXTERNAL: FROM THE SYSTEM PERSPECTIVE

In our experience, most instructional coaches are hired from within the district, typically from the teaching pool. Indeed, in many districts, posting the position internally is a first step before posting it externally. Internal recruitment of coaches involves one or more of the following approaches (Society for Human Resource Management [SHRM], 2021c):

» Internal job posting
» Encouragement from the candidate's supervisor or coworkers
» A list of employees interested in particular positions
» Succession planning as vacancies in coaching roles arise

Many school districts ask employees to complete annual letters of intent, in which they indicate a willingness to remain in their current roles, the desire to apply for a new role, or the intention to leave the district. The data from letters of intent aid districts in planning for turnover and in seeing what the candidate pool may look like for various roles. Still, the tangible evidence of a new role that comes with the release of a new job posting can result in increased interest in the job and is an important internal marketing function.

When recruiting external talent, the HR department takes on an additional marketing role. School district HR departments commonly use job fairs and other traditional external recruitment methods for teaching positions, but coaching positions may require more targeted methods such as placing ads on job-search apps and websites and on social media sites and listservs.

Because districts often require that instructional coaches assist teachers in using various strategies and programs aligned with the district's instructional framework, districts understandably have a greater level of comfort with hiring coaches from within their existing teaching ranks. That said, seeking external candidates can bring valuable new perspectives to the coaching role and enhance the diversity of experience and viewpoints in the coaching program.

INTERNAL VERSUS EXTERNAL: FROM THE SCHOOL PERSPECTIVE

A more common question we hear from school districts about internal versus external candidates involves whether to hire a coach in a school in which they have not previously worked as a teacher or whether to hire a coach from among the teachers in the same school building. Hiring the coach from within the school is tempting, particularly if a candidate for the role has very positive relationships with and a solid reputation among the school's teachers, but the issue is not that simple.

Trouble can arise within the school when that teacher assumes the role of instructional coach. Other teachers who wanted that role may resent the coach, but, more important, the change in title and function can change the relationships between the coach and colleagues in the building. Now that the coach must build relationships more intentionally and consistently with *everyone* as a function of her work, she can no longer engage in some conversations or vent frustrations as she may have done in the past with friends on the staff. That is, coaches have a different ethical mandate to maintain confidentiality with the teachers they coach and to treat everyone as a partner. Old friends may react negatively to the coach's new ways, and that may lead to the perception of the coach as someone who is "not our friend anymore."

Hiring coaches from other school buildings largely eliminates that problem, but it has its own challenges in terms of relationship building. When Sharon applied for her district's first school-specific high school instructional coach role, she very much hoped that the school chosen for that pilot role would be the one where she had taught for 13 years. She loved her school and the school community, and didn't want to leave. When the role was assigned to a different high school, she decided that she still wanted it because she wanted to support teachers more deeply as part of her work.

Because many people in the new building had met her before at district-wide activities and events, Sharon was not a total stranger to most of the teachers in her new school. But she still had to build rapport and relationships with them—they all needed to get to know each other—and relationship building was a huge part of the job, especially in the first year. On the positive side, in the new school, Sharon had no preexisting deep and complex relationships that required redefining, and that was helpful. On reflection, Sharon is glad that the role wasn't assigned to her original school. She quickly loved her new school community, too, and it was definitely easier to start fresh in a new environment than to reinvent parts of herself for the old one.

PASSIVE JOBS SEEKERS VERSUS ACTIVE JOB SEEKERS

HR research and literature often describe the difference between recruiting that focuses on active versus passive job seekers (SHRM, 2021a, 2021c). Active job seekers are people who are not content with their current jobs for whatever reason, whereas "[p]assive job seekers are individuals who are currently employed and not actively looking for a new job, but who may be open to a good career opportunity if one came along" (SHRM, 2021a, p. 1). Most employers prefer passive job seekers because they like the idea of hiring people who are happy in their work and who presumably have a positive job history (SHRM, 2021c).

When it comes to instructional coaching, both active and passive job seekers could be excellent candidates. Administrators and fellow teachers may encourage passive job seekers to apply for the role, but others may have a definite interest in being a coach and may be eagerly waiting for such a job posting to arise.

One concern for us with regard to active job seekers involves educators who perceive an instructional coaching role as a step up on the career ladder that will help them to garner some other role in the system later on. The best coaches are people who genuinely want to support adults and enjoy working with adults as partners in student growth. Someone who views the coach role primarily as a "promotion" on the way to a more formal leadership role may not have a partnership approach as their focus and may not have much interest in the time and effort it takes to build relationships across a school or district to foster deep coaching work.

Jim describes the five factors most associated with trusting relationships in *Better Conversations* (Knight, 2016):

1. Honesty
2. Reliability
3. Competence
4. Warmth
5. Stewardship

For coaches to act in a spirit of stewardship means that they take a "servant leadership" approach to supporting others because service is the right thing to do, not because they are seeking some other role or some reward for that service. If coaches view the job as one they need to "check off the list" on their way to other jobs, they jeopardize their ability to foster stewardship, and thus trust, and therefore the deep change that can come through coaching.

Nevertheless, being an instructional coach is terrific preparation for becoming the kind of an administrator who builds community and promotes professional learning. We would not want to exclude anyone from coaching because they have administrative ambitions.

But we do want to ensure that, right now, a given candidate wants to be an instructional coach—a candidate who wants to support teachers deeply as a partner.

To try to determine whether a candidate's primary focus is coaching or future administrative positions, hiring managers could include questions in the screening interview such as, "Where do you see yourself in the system in the next few years? What about in 5-10 years?" Another strategy for identifying candidates who may not see coaching as a role in which they plan to invest much time is to provide as much clarity as possible about what the role and the coaching approach entail in the job description and in all materials associated with the coaching role. The clearer the district is about what coaches do and what they don't do, the more candidates can "screen themselves" to decide whether the role is in line with their skills and goals.

MANAGING THE CANDIDATE EXPERIENCE

One other consideration in developing a strong, diverse, and qualified candidate pool is to make the "candidate experience a consistent and standardized process that respects the candidate and makes the process simple and even pleasant," or what SHRM calls "managing the candidate experience" (SHRM, 2021c, p. 5). According to SHRM, "How a candidate is treated from the earliest stages of submitting his or her resume/application through the in-person interviews to the offer/decline process are all considered part of the candidate experience" (p. 5). The more helpfully and respectfully the HR department and hiring managers plan for that experience, the more likely they are to engage good candidates for the position.

SHRM (2021c) recommends focusing on the following four areas to provide candidates with what they need:

1. **RESUME/APPLICATION SUBMISSION:** Be sure that the written materials clearly communicate the job skills and requirements and that submitting any materials is an easy process to navigate.

2. **CANDIDATE COMMUNICATION:** Provide clear and timely communication regarding when applications have been accepted, the status of interviews, and any answers to candidate questions.

3. **INTERVIEWER INTERACTIONS:** Prepare thoroughly for the interviews, review the candidate's application in advance, be respectful of candidate responses and questions, and show consideration for the candidate's time.

4. **CANDIDATE LOGISTICS:** Provide candidates with clear instructions regarding the logistics for their visits to an interview site.

After the hiring manager and HR have established the hiring process and the recruitment strategy, they can then advertise the position accordingly. Once candidates apply, new work begins—narrowing the field through the interview process.

Helpful Interview Processes

Adam Grant, in his *Work Life* podcast (2020a), says that "Job interviews as you know them are broken." Grant maintains that employers are stuck in the past and that hiring managers are lagging in their use of science to guide good hiring practices that lead to choosing the best people. We see this problem in the hiring of instructional coaches out in the field.

Hiring managers can have an inflated sense of their ability to "read" people and feel that they can tell whom they should hire for a given role from just a single conversation. In schools, if a teacher has a stellar reputation for his work in the classroom and a positive rapport with administrators, leaders may view an instructional coaching role for that teacher as an "inevitability" rather than something he needs to demonstrate he can do. After one quick interview, that teacher is usually hired. The trouble is, Grant (2020a) tells us, that most interview processes don't involve the steps they need to ensure that the right person steps into the role, and he views the problem as having three facets.

» **PROBLEM 1:** Candidates may not respond to interviews authentically. Comedian Chris Rock sums it up nicely: "Interviewers aren't meeting you. They're meeting your representative" (as cited in Grant, 2020a). Because of the way most hiring managers approach interviews, candidates tell interviewers what they want to hear, an edited version of the truth. They don't demonstrate who they are and how well their skills and experience align with the job description. In such cases, job interviews may be no more revelatory or helpful than a Facebook post, in which the goal is usually to charm, to humor, or to get "Likes."

Good interview processes and questions aligned with the job, on the other hand, help to elicit more authentic responses that will be helpful in making the hiring decision. According to SHRM (2021b), "If done effectively, the interview enables the employer to determine if an applicant's skills, experience and personality meet the job's requirements" (p. 2), not merely how affable they are.

» **PROBLEM 2:** Interviewers need to ask better questions. Grant (2020a) explains that, so often, interview questions focus on things that have nothing to do with the job. For an interview to be relevant and helpful, hiring managers need to identify the "key values and skills needed for the job." Also, in asking questions directly related to the role and to the workplace, interviewers will help to "level the playing field" for candidates with less experience but who may have great potential in a given role.

> » **PROBLEM 3:** Interviewer bias typically goes unchecked in interviews. Some hiring managers describe making hiring decisions with "their gut" rather than with evidence about candidates, not realizing that they may be making the hiring decision with a high level of personal bias. Too often, Grant (2020a) points out, employers focus on common interests with candidates instead of common values. Common values (integrity, autonomy, education, professional growth, etc.) lead to better team cohesion, coordination, and commitment, which enhances performance and retention. Common interests (books, music, athletics, etc.), on the other hand, may break down by age, gender, class, cultural background, and other areas where bias can creep into the hiring decision.

This issue of bias in interviews is usually unintentional and demands attention. According to Grant (2020a), a pervasive workplace focus on the "culture fit" of candidates can lead to hiring people with similar experiences and backgrounds (itself a form of bias) instead of people who share important values that serve the mission of the organization. Therefore, Grant (2020a) encourages employers to focus on the candidate's potential "culture contribution" instead of their "fit"; in other words, employers should focus on what candidates can add to the organization's professional culture, not on whether they already conform to it.

To prevent the problems presented by Grant during instructional coach interviews and to make interviews the best possible environments in which to get to know the candidates, we recommend a careful, threefold approach consisting of

1. Choosing the interview team
2. Choosing the interview format
3. Choosing the interview questions

CHOOSING THE INTERVIEW TEAM

Most hiring managers use some sort of screening process (especially if many people have applied for the role) followed by more in-depth interviews. Usually, HR handles the screening interviews, but people who know the coach role more deeply should be involved in the other interviews. In schools, group interviews are common because the various job roles affect so many different stakeholders.

GROUP INTERVIEW APPROACHES

Typically, hiring managers choose one of two types of group interview approaches—a candidate group interview or a panel group interview. "In a candidate group interview, a candidate is in a room with other job applicants who may be applying for the same position" (SHRM, 2021b, p. 4). The candidate may move from interviewer to interviewer in those rooms, with each team member focused on a different element of the job. (SHRM, 2021b). The second type, the panel interview, involves a single candidate interviewed by a panel of two or more people. "This type of group interview is usually a question-and-answer session, but a candidate may also be asked to participate in an exercise or test" (SHRM, 2021b, p. 4).

USING THE TEAM TO REDUCE BIAS

Whether hiring managers decide to use candidate-group interviews, panel-group interviews, or both, one way to limit bias in the interviews is to select interview team members who represent a diverse set of roles, experiences, and perspectives. Having different kinds of people on the team acknowledges a truth that few want to admit: Everyone has biases.

When Sharon attended a Candidate Support Provider training from the National Board for Professional Teaching Standards (NBPTS) years ago, the facilitators discussed at length the bias issues related to scoring National Board Certification candidates. They explained that everyone has biases and that the key to fair scoring is for scorers to acknowledge their biases and monitor them during scoring. If a scorer is biased in favor of elementary school environments, for example, then they need to be aware of that when scoring secondary teachers. If a scorer is biased against the idea of students being seated in desks that are lined up in rows, then they need to be aware of that bias when scoring, too. Being aware of our biases is the first step toward preventing them from influencing our behavior toward others. Monitoring our behavior with our biases in mind is the second step.

Most of us think of ourselves as extremely fair and unbiased. Even while those NBPTS facilitators were explaining how pervasive bias is, and that *everyone has biases*, Sharon was thinking, "Well, I would never let something like that influence me in scoring." Grant, in his book *Think Again* (2021), explains this denial: "My favorite bias is the 'I'm not biased' bias in which people believe they are more objective than others. It turns out that smart people are more likely to fall into this trap. The brighter you are, the harder it can be to see your own limitations. Being good at thinking can make you worse at rethinking" (p. 25).

One challenge in understanding our biases is that we may think of bias solely in terms of demographics, such as race, gender, religion, national origin, age, and socioeconomic level. But bias is a multi-faceted villain and takes many forms. For example, some hiring managers may have the bias that employees should "come up the ladder" in the same way that they did and, therefore, relate more to candidates who are following their own career path than to candidates who are not. Other hiring managers may have a bias for or against particular universities that candidates attended, and still others may have a referral bias that causes them to "go easy" on a candidate in an interview because they respect the person who referred the candidate for the job.

Because bias is so pervasive and because hiring managers are often unaware of what their own biases are, having a diverse interview team encourages multiple perspectives in the hiring conversations and can prevent one person's biases from influencing the hiring decision.

CHOOSING THE INTERVIEW FORMAT

Once the interview team is in place, deciding on the interview format is next. Jim has long recommended a multi-step process for interviewing instructional coach candidates. His process involves four separate interviews, with each one further narrowing the field of candidates (Knight, 2022). We suggest a "structured interview" approach in which all candidates are asked the same questions. This best practice "makes it easier for the interviewer to evaluate and compare applicants fairly" and "can be crucial in defending against allegations of discrimination in hiring and selection, because all applicants are asked the same questions" (SHRM, 2021b, p. 2).

AN INTERVIEW PROCESS FOR INSTRUCTIONAL COACHES

We first describe the basics of each of the four interviews, and in Choosing the Interview Questions, we provide specific guidance on types of questions to ask in each type of interview.

Step 1: Screening interview.
The screening interview allows hiring managers to quickly eliminate candidates who are not qualified or appropriate for the role in some way. These interviews are usually one-to-one over the telephone or

in an online meeting forum. Screening interviews typically include "knockout questions," which is HR industry slang for questions that have clear right or wrong answers, and in which the wrong answers "knock the candidate out" of consideration for the job.

Step 2: Skills interview.

Once the screening interview has narrowed the field of candidates, the skills interview is next. For instructional coaches, questions in this interview may involve issues such as curriculum, teaching, and coaching, but Jim recommends that at least 50% of the questions relate to foundational skills in interpersonal communication, in which the candidates describe how they have navigated such things as building trusting relationships and handling conflict.

Questions in the skills interview are typically a blend of

» **BEHAVIORAL QUESTIONS** (e.g., "Give me a specific example of a time when you used good judgment and logic in solving a problem"; SHRM, 2021b, p. 3),

» **COMPETENCY-BASED QUESTIONS** (e.g., "Tell me about a time when you had to encourage others to contribute ideas or opinions. How did you get everyone to contribute? What was the end result?"), and

» **SITUATIONAL QUESTIONS** (e.g., "You are a new coach leading your first PD session for teachers on a back-to-school day. What will you do during that session to build trust, make connections, and clarify what your role is and is not?").

Step 3: Model interview.

The skills interview will likely narrow the candidate field even more. The small number of candidates remaining will next engage in demonstrating a teaching strategy for the interview panel. The candidates will receive the materials for a strategy that they have not used before, and they will have one day to learn that strategy before coming in to model it, with the inter-view panel acting as teachers who are learning the strategy.

In Jim's experience with this type of modeling exercise, candi-dates distinguish themselves from each other in the ability to learn quickly, in the ability to be clear in explaining teaching strategies, in their energy levels, in how well they work under pressure, and how they cope with a situation that is outside their comfort zone (Knight, 2022).

Sometimes situational questions during the skills interview come in the form of hypothetical scenarios to which the candidate must respond, but the modeling task goes deeper, into an actual demon-stration. All interviews have limitations in terms of time and scope, so although the modeling interview appears to be more focused on implementation support than on Impact Cycle coaching, it can quickly reveal some important characteristics that help to identify the best candidate. At this stage of the hiring process, the inter-view panel needs to see the final candidates *doing something*, not just responding to interview questions. Because a coach's inter-personal skills and approach with adults are so crucial to success, the time and energy that hiring managers invest in this type of interview will likely reveal the best candidates for the role.

Step 4: References interview.
The final interview does not involve the candidates directly; instead, this is the time when the hiring manager interviews the candidate's references. References are most helpful as a tool to confirm the candidate's responses to any written application materials and to their responses in interviews.

References have a low level of validity and reliability in terms of providing good information about candidates, particularly when they are in the form of letters (Noe et al., 2008). Speaking with references yields better information. Providing poor references for a candidate can make a reference subject to lawsuits for libel (Noe et al., 2008), so hiring managers need to keep conversations fact-based, evidence-based, and directly tied to job skills to give the reference a sense of safety in speaking about a given candidate. Hiring managers should avoid contacting anyone who is not named on the reference list about the candidate without first obtaining permission from the candidate.

CHOOSING THE INTERVIEW QUESTIONS

Working as a team to prepare questions for each of the four types of interviews reduces bias in the questions, ensures consistency in questioning among candidates, and gives everyone a clearer process focused on the actual job skills and requirements.

QUESTIONS FOR THE SCREENING INTERVIEW

Screening interviews are designed to eliminate applicants who are unable or unwilling to perform key job functions, lack required qualifications, or exhibit other red flags. Usually a single person conducts these interviews (either an HR professional or the hiring manager). The interview team, in consultation with HR, should determine the screening questions in advance and focus on issues that would clearly rule out a candidate from consideration.

The screening interview may involve asking questions to clarify skills and experience that the candidate provided on the application materials. Questions may also target aspects of the job that are non-negotiable, such as

» "This job requires working a duty day that starts at 7:00 am and ends at 4:00 pm. Are you able to do that?"
» "This role is multi-school and requires that you be able to travel to different buildings during the duty day. Are you able to do that?"

» "Your application indicates that you have worked as a licensed teacher for several years, but because you're not currently employed by our district, will you provide us with documentation of your teaching licensure?"

QUESTIONS FOR THE SKILLS INTERVIEW

The skills interview's purpose is to determine whether the candidate has the ability to form the job functions. Here, the interview team is primarily examining candidates' emotional intelligence. Patton (2018) describes emotional intelligence as "a competency that measures an individual's ability to do the following three things:

» **RECOGNIZE**. Candidates with high self-recognition will know what they are good at. They know their triggers, moods, personality type and communication style.

» **READ.** The candidate has situational awareness, which is the ability to walk into a room and know the mood before anyone speaks.

» **RESPOND.** The candidate can respond appropriately to a situation." (p. 1)

Elements of emotional intelligence to look for in interviews include the following (Patton, 2018):

» Self-awareness
» Empathy
» Self-control
» Stress tolerance
» Flexibility
» Optimism

To measure these characteristics, some combination of behavioral, competency-based, and situational questions is helpful.

Behavioral and competency-based questions.

"Behavioral and competency-based interviewing both aim to discover how the interviewee performed in specific situations. The logic is based on the principle that past performance predicts future behavior; how the applicant behaved in the past indicates how he or she will behave in the future" (SHRM, 2021b, p. 3). Examples of behavioral and competency-based questions for instructional coaches include the following:

» Tell us about a conflict you've had with a coworker and how you resolved it.

» How would the teachers in your school describe you?

» What do you do when someone resists your ideas at work?

» Walk us through a meeting you've led from to start to finish.

» When was the last time you changed your mind about something at work?

» What is your favorite failure at work?

» If you could go back a few years, what advice would you give your younger self about working with adults?

» Describe a situation where you had to share difficult information with a colleague or you disagreed with a colleague. How did you handle that conversation?

» Describe a time when you refused to compromise on your values at work.

Situational questions.

 A situational question gives "the candidate a hypothetical scenario or event and focuses on his or her past experiences, behaviors, knowledge, skills and abilities by asking the candidate to provide specific examples of how the candidate would respond given the situation described" (SHRM, 2021b, p. 4). These questions remove candidates from the real-world examples they gave in the behavioral and competency-based questions and ask them to troubleshoot a new scenario that they may face as a coach. Examples of situational questions include the following:

» How would you go about getting to know people in your new school?

» What measures might you use to determine your success as a coach?

Interviewers may want to provide candidates with more specific scenarios than those in the questions above to give candidates more context and detail. Hearing different candidate's responses to specific scenarios can enable the interview team to note more subtle differences among the candidates' approach and judgment. Hiring managers may want to create scenarios for this purpose using actual situations they have navigated with other coaches. In the box, we provide five sample scenarios that hiring managers can modify to suit their needs.

INSTRUCTIONAL COACHING SCENARIOS

SCENARIO 1

After teaching language arts for many years, Travon is a new instructional coach in the middle school where he taught. Because he had always had positive relationships with his colleagues in the school, he's surprised that few of them are asking for his support in the classroom. A couple of friends in the building have told him that rumors abound that he is in the coach role to report what's really happening in classrooms to school and district administrators. To build more trusting relationships in the building, what should be his next steps?

SCENARIO 2

Keysha, a coach in an elementary school, has been working on a classroom management goal with Stacy for several weeks. Before the coaching cycle began, Stacy's fourth graders were only on task for an average of 60% of the class time, and inappropriate behaviors were so frequent that she was not able to correct them consistently or fluently. Since working with Keysha on teaching routines and expectations, on-task behaviors in the class have improved, but consistent corrections have not. When examining the data, Stacy says, "Well, most of those problem behaviors come from three students, and they don't respond to correction, so I just give up with them. They come from such bad homes and tough neighborhoods that there's nothing I can do about it. I'll just keep writing office referrals for them until the principal finally gets them out of here." Keysha does not share Stacy's perspective about the students or what is in their best interests. What should Keysha do?

SCENARIO 3

Maya is an instructional coach in a high school. When she first started coaching two years ago, she and her principal, Jenni, reviewed the tasks she needed to perform as a coach and how much of her workday she should devote to each task. Since then, Maya regularly tracks her time on each task to make sure she is holding up her end of the agreement. Because part of her job involves providing district-level PD for teachers, she is increasingly out of her school building to report to district-level administrators for those PD sessions. As a result, she feels like she is not providing enough support to teachers who have asked for coaching. Jenni is also expressing concern about how much time district administrators are asking from Maya. Maya feels like she is being pulled in all directions and is not doing right by anyone. What should Maya do to improve the situation?

SCENARIO 4

Michael is a district-wide social studies coach in three high schools. His district has worked hard over the past two years to remove anything from coaches' duties that appears to be quasi-administrative in nature (fidelity checks, reporting to principals on teachers' performance improvement plans, etc.) to foster a partnership approach so that teachers feel safer in asking coaches for deeper classroom support. Nonetheless, teachers are frequently

asking Michael for feedback on their performance, and that makes
him feel very uncomfortable. He wants to give teachers what they
think they need, but he doesn't want teachers to view him as a
junior assistant principal. What should he do?

SCENARIO 5

As part of her coaching work with math teachers around the
district, Valerie is assisting them with implementing a new textbook program. Teachers already felt overwhelmed by all of the
new things they've had to juggle this year, so the new textbook has
made them feel even more anxious. Early on, Valerie had offered
teachers support in the form of modeling lessons in their classrooms from the new materials. What she is seeing now, though, is
that some teachers appear to be asking for modeling not because
they want to learn the textbook program more deeply but because
they want Valerie's modeling to function as a form of "class
coverage" so that they can have a break. Some teachers have even
asked Valerie to model full 90-minute blocks of class time. Valerie
wants to support teachers and to be flexible, but she's concerned
about this reaction. What should she do?

QUESTIONS FOR THE MODEL INTERVIEW

As we describe in the previous section of the chapter, the
model interview should involve giving the final candidates
a new teaching strategy to learn and asking them to demonstrate its use to an audience of "teachers" the following day.
Clarity around the directions for this task is imperative to
allow candidates to do their best work during the demonstration and not make deciphering the guidelines an additional
stressor for them. In addition to written instructions, the hiring
manager should explain the task to each candidate verbally

and encourage them to ask questions. A sample prompt may look something like this:

Enclosed please find the teacher's guide and resources box for the JAMS Discussion Strategy, a classroom discussion technique for students in grades 7-12. Examine these materials and complete any reading, practice, or research you may feel you need in order to be prepared to model and demonstrate Lesson 1 to the "teachers" in your session (the interview panel) tomorrow at 4:00 pm in the board office conference room. Here are the logistical parameters for your demonstration of that teaching strategy:

1.   You will begin demonstrating Lesson 1 at 4:10 pm and must complete the lesson by 4:30 pm. You may engage the "teachers" and require their participation as you would any real-life adult learners in this type of lesson modeling.

2.   You will have the use of an interactive whiteboard, projector, speakers, and Internet access during the lesson should you need them.

3.   Afterward, you will have time to reflect and debrief with the panel on why you approached the lesson as you did and discuss any areas for your future growth in learning the strategy.

Providing the candidates with autonomy within these parameters will help the panel to see how the candidates work with adults, their skill in taking on new approaches, and their ability to reflect on their practice and target areas for improvement. All of these issues go right to the heart of effective instructional coaching.

An additional (and optional) layer to this fourth interview stage would be to engage the final candidates in one-to-one coaching conversations in which a member of the interview panel acts as the "teacher" and the candidate is the "coach." This additional demonstration may be especially helpful in cases where a clearly "best" candidate is not yet apparent or if interview panel members would like to see a one-to-one conversation in a different scenario than the ones that already took place in the interview process. Some types of one-to-one coaching conversations that could be prompts for this activity are

» Using Growth Coaching International's GROWTH questions (Campbell & van Nieuwerburgh, 2018)

» Using Michael Bungay Stanier's coaching questions from The Coaching Habit (Stanier, 2016)

» Asking the candidate to explain a teaching strategy to the "teacher" using a checklist as Jim describes in *The Impact Cycle* (Knight, 2017)

PLANNING FOR THE INTERVIEWS

The hiring manager, HR, and the interview team can ensure a helpful and humanizing interview process with careful planning. For the screening interviews, the hiring manager and HR can meet to determine which job requirements and skills are "make or break" for candidates. Either the hiring manager or an HR professional is likely to be the person who conducts those interviews without participation by the interview panel.

For all subsequent interviews, the hiring manager, HR, and the interview panel will act as a team. That team approach involves multiple perspectives and personalities, which is certainly a benefit, but it can also bring inconsistency and a lack of cohesion to the process as well. Having the team meet in advance of the interview to determine questions, to examine issues of bias, and to determine scoring criteria candidate responses can eliminate those problems.

To aid districts in this process, Appendix 8\APP8\ is an Instructional Coach Candidate Evaluation Form that can serve as a starting point for those conversations. When the skills interview and the model interview involve questions aligned with the standards on the evaluation form, the team ensures that interviews remain focused on the job itself and avoid bias. The questions that the team creates to align with those standards can take multiple forms (direct questions, scenarios, aspects of the model interview, etc.) and involve a variety of possible "good" answers from candidates. The important thing is that the team is consistent in how it approaches the interviews and the scoring process so that they are following best hiring practices and can determine the best candidate for the job.

With the four different interview situations and with careful planning, the hope is that candidates won't end up feeling as if the interviews were akin to "interrogations." Job candidates and instructional coaches are people too, and they respond best to supportive environments in which everyone wants them to succeed. Yes, each interview is intended to narrow the candidate field, but each interview can also be a chance for candidates to demonstrate their strengths and their willingness to learn and grow.

For interviewers, to create humanizing interview environments, withholding judgment (especially "in the moment") is crucial. Keeping an open mind and considering their responses before judging candidates will aid in keeping the conversations positive, focused on the coaching role, and reassuring for the candidates. As SHRM (2021b) says, "the employer should not go into an interview with a list of ideal answers in mind. It is unlikely that any applicant would come close to providing such answers. A better approach is to keep in mind ideal characteristics that a successful candidate would possess" (p. 5). Staying focused on the coaching role ensures more fairness, more professionalism, and a higher likelihood that the truly best candidate will become clear to everyone.

CONTINUOUS QUESTION IMPROVEMENT

The workplace is a living, changing thing. Some workplace attitudes and behaviors that were appropriate 30 or 40 years ago may not be appropriate now. Because job interviews should be engaging and humanizing learning experiences for everyone, continuing to examine the questions that hiring managers ask candidates is important.

In Jim's book on the Seven Success Factors (Knight, 2022), he lists some of the questions that he has used over the years in coach interviews. As we delved into the HR research for this book, we discovered that some of those questions would benefit from revision or deletion. None of the original questions arose from ill intent of any kind. It's just that times have changed, and we believe in changing with them, especially when it comes to ensuring the equitable treatment of all candidates.

Below is the list of interview questions that Jim used in the past but showing the edits we have made since that book was published. (Deletions are marked with ~~strike-through~~, and additions are shown in **boldface**.

SAMPLE INTERVIEW QUESTIONS

» Tell us about a conflict you've had **with a coworker** and how you resolved it.

» ~~What kind of people do you struggle to get along with?~~

» How would you go about getting to know people in your new school?

» What do you need to do to be a better communicator **at work**?

» What **professional learning** book or **resource have you found most valuable in your work** ~~is the last book you read that really changed you~~?

» How **would the teachers in your school** ~~do other people~~ describe you?

» Describe the **professional** learning you've done in the past year and how it's affected your practice.

» What do you do when someone resists your ideas **at work**?

» Walk us through a meeting you've led from to start to finish.

» What measures might you use to determine your success as a coach?

» What brings you joy **at work**?

» ~~What do you do for fun when you're not working?~~

Additional questions that we chose specifically for the current book received the same treatment:

» When was the last time you changed your mind about something **at work**?

» What is your favorite failure **at work**?

» If you could go back a few years, what advice would you give your younger self **about working with adults**?

» Describe a situation where you had to share difficult information with a colleague or you disagreed with a colleague? How did you handle that conversation?

» Describe a time when you refused to compromise on your values **at work**?

Note that most of the edits involved tying the sentence directly to the workplace. Questions that involve (or could be interpreted as involving) situations outside of work can be great for "getting-to-know-you" conversations once the new employee has been hired. But during the interview process, staying focused on the job and its relevant skills keeps the attention where it needs to be. Focusing on the job also avoids opening the door to personal information that can make some candidates uncomfortable and potentially result in accusations of bias from candidates who didn't get the job. "The bottom line is: When interviewing job candidates, employers should stay focused on the job being interviewed for and determine if candidates meet the criteria for that position.

Anything beyond that could be venturing into unwelcome and potentially litigious territory" (Onley, 2021, p. 2). For a listing of all of the questions without the editorial marks, see the box below.

SAMPLE INSTRUCTIONAL COACH INTERVIEW QUESTIONS

» Tell us about a conflict you've had with a coworker and how you resolved it.

» How would you go about getting to know people in your new school?

» What do you need to do to become a better communicator at work?

» What professional learning book or resource have you found most valuable in your work?

» How would the teachers in your school describe you?

» Describe the professional learning you've done in the past year and how it has affected your practice.

» What do you do when someone resists your ideas at work?

» Walk us through a meeting you've led from to start to finish.

» What measures might you use to determine your success as a coach?

» What brings you joy at work?

» When was the last time you changed your mind about something at work?

» What is your favorite failure at work?

» If you could go back a few years, what advice would you give your younger self about working with adults?

» Describe a situation where you had to share difficult information with a colleague or you disagreed with a colleague? How did you handle that conversation?

» Describe a time when you refused to compromise on your values at work?

Bias can be deeply ingrained in all of us, so hiring managers and interview team members need training and practice in forming interview questions and in practicing interview scenarios. Becoming aware of one's biases and developing skill in eliminating them from our day-to-day interactions is challenging work that takes focused attention and practice for everyone.

MAKING THE HIRING DECISION

Creating a four-part interview structure like this takes time and significant attention to detail. But the structure ensures a level of thoroughness that is essential in determining which candidates are the best people for the job. If this process has done its job, then by the end of the model interviews, a "best" candidate for the job should be clear to the interview team. When that happens, the hiring manager's job is easy—make the job offer to that candidate. When the best candidate is not as obvious, the hiring manager must take into account several factors to pick the first-choice candidate by

» reviewing the panel's scoring of each interview for each finalist against the job requirements
» reviewing the qualifications and experience of each finalist against the job requirements
» reflecting on each candidate's emotional intelligence as demonstrated during the hiring process
» determining which candidates may bring a new cultural contribution to the group

To aid districts in using the data from each part of the hiring process, we created an Instructional Coach Candidate Evaluation Form (Appendix 8) as a candidate rubric. The form is organized around the Seven Success Factors to ensure the alignment of the coach role to the hiring decision. Hiring managers can use our form as the starting point for their own form and should consider potential modifications to it based on their coaches' duties and their candidate pool:

» Do you need to take into account how you will score veteran coaches differently than new candidates on the rubric to ensure fairness while also indentifying candidates who may have less coaching experience but who are very promising in the role?
» Do you need to add other coaching duties to the form beyond the ones described in the Seven Success Factors?
» Should the hiring manager weigh some of the elements on the form more heavily than others in making the hiring decision?

Once the hiring manager, HR, and members of the interview panel have each completed this form for each candidate, the hiring manager can enter all of the scores into a spreadsheet to enable comparison of the candidates across the different domains. Even at this final stage of the hiring process, the emphasis is still on clarity regarding what effective coaches do and which candidates' skills best align with those traits.

Consultation with HR or other colleagues may be useful, but in the end, the hiring manager must focus the hiring decision on which candidate's skills are most in line with the requirements of the job. Hiring decisions are one of the most challenging responsibilities for leaders, and for good reason. Every hiring decision is, at least to some extent, a strong, "educated guess" at the candidate's potential in the role. The key is to take every possible step to ensure that the decision is more "educated" and less "guess" in relation to the standards of best instructional coaching practice.

ᴐᴌᴌ

In examining the research on hiring practices across industries, one thing has become clear to us: Hiring is one of the most difficult tasks a leader has to perform, yet most leaders have not received the training and resources they need to do that job well. Our hope with this chapter is that, by using the processes and resources we suggest, leaders will not only be using best coaching practices to choose coaches but also best HR practices to hire employees.

Focusing solely on the legalities of hiring is the minimum standard in hiring situations. But as with every facet of this book, we want more than the minimum. We want hiring of instructional coaches to involve a process that results in the best candidates for the role, that is humanizing for everyone involved (the candidates, the interview panel, the hiring manager, and HR), and that communicates fully and deeply what instructional coaches do. To do that requires putting aside perceptions and past history and instead focusing on the job and the hiring process. Focusing on the job, in this case, means focusing on what works best for teachers and students, and that is always best practice.

NOTES

 # To Sum Up:

By using the specific, research-based elements of instructional coaching to guide the recruitment, interviews, and hiring of instructional coaches, districts ensure that the best candidates apply for the job and that the best candidates for those roles are selected.

⬡ Making It Real:

To make recruiting and hiring of instructional coaches real, reach out to the HR professionals in your district. If you are new to the job of hiring coaches, ask them about what that process has looked like in the past and make suggestions for how you would like it to change in the future. Examine issues of recruitment, interviewing, and hiring to ensure that everyone is communicating clearly about coaching.

To apply these concepts directly to your work with hiring coaches, consider two additional elements to the process we've described. First, at the earliest stages of the hiring process, seek input from teachers about what they need in an instructional coach to give the interview panel valuable information that can inform the job description, the interview questions, and other elements of hiring. Providing teachers with a voice in the process and hearing their real needs will make everyone more engaged when the coaching work begins. Second, videotaping the interviews with candidates not only makes the interview process more efficient for everyone but also provides a professional learning opportunity for the interview panel. Panel members can use the video to examine whether they think any unintentional biases crept into the interview questions, whether interviewer body language sent any unintended messages to candidates, etc. Reflection on hiring practices in this way promotes continuous improvement in making hiring practices the best they can be.

Reflection Questions:

What was most valuable in this chapter?

....

....

....

....

....

....

What are the benefits of the way you hire instructional coaches now?

....

....

....

....

....

....

What are some of the problems you see with your current hiring practices for instructional coaches?

....

....

....

....

....

....

Which elements of research-based coaching would you like to add to your hiring practices?

....

....

....

....

....

Which hiring processes are already in place and/or required by your HR department?

....

....

....

....

....

....

Would our suggested four-part interview process be helpful in determining who the best coach candidates are?

....

....

....

....

....

....

Going Deeper:

The four-stage interview process described in this chapter was inspired by Geoff Smart and Randy Street's book *Who* (2008). The book is written for the corporate world, so not all of its ideas apply to a social sector, but it includes many tools that are useful to anyone hiring employees. Jennifer Eberhardt's *Biased* (2019) will help any reader see how their implicit biases shape the way they see people and the world. It should be compulsory reading for anyone who says, "I'm not biased." And speaking of rethinking how we see the world, Adam Grant's *Think Again* (2021) beautifully makes the case that to do what we do well, we need to unlearn just as much as we learn. Finally, for a different perspective on work in general, read James Suzmans' *Work* (2020), which starts out with a history of work from "the stone to the age of robots" as the subtitle promises, but ends by prompting us to question many of our assumptions about the purpose of work and what it means to each individual.

CHAPTER 5

RETAINING COACHES AND SUSTAINING COACHING PROGRAMS

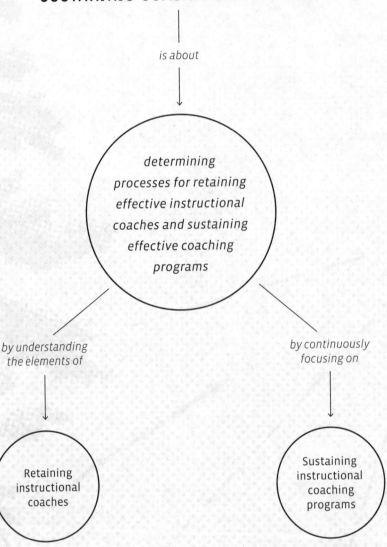

is about

determining processes for retaining effective instructional coaches and sustaining effective coaching programs

by understanding the elements of

by continuously focusing on

Retaining instructional coaches

Sustaining instructional coaching programs

- Emphasizing employee engagement
- Developing strong coach-supervisor relationships
- Providing professional learning opportunities
- Developing a coach retention plan

- Consciously developing the professional culture
- Supporting the coaching champion
- Evaluating the program to make improvements

CHAPTER

05

RETAINING COACHES AND

SUSTAINING COACHING PROGRAMS

 SNAPSHOT:

This chapter suggests ways to strengthen coach

retention and coaching program sustainability. It

synthesizes the ideas from chapters 1-4 to aid leaders

in developing the strongest instructional coaching

programs possible.

Maria was ready for a change. After many years as a teacher, she wanted a new challenge to help her grow as a professional. When she saw a job posting in her district for a middle school literacy coach, she enthusiastically applied, even though the posting involved no real job description or listing of coaching tasks.

During her interview with Finlay, the principal, after a brief review of her resume, she was surprised by how quickly they went from, "Hello. How are you?" to "Maria, as far as I'm concerned, you've got the job." When Maria asked about exactly what the job entailed, Finlay said, "We're not really sure yet. Besides teaching a couple of reading intervention classes, I don't really know what you'll be doing, but welcome aboard!" Maria wasn't sure what to make of that comment, but because "other duties as assigned" is an accepted way of life in schools, she thought, "OK, we'll just figure it out as we go."

Maria's "office" was one of those relocatable classrooms (a "portable," in teacher slang) that are detached from the rest of the building. Out there alone with her two reading intervention classes, she sensed that she should be working to connect with other teachers, perhaps developing programs or professional development (PD) resources for them, but no one had articulated any kind of vision or plan for that.

Always a go-getter, Maria took matters into her own hands and started advertising "lunch and learn" literacy sessions in the media center. She brought some food, set out some resources, and hoped that teachers would come and see what she had to offer. Some did; most didn't. She sent out emails to the teachers asking to visit their classrooms and watch them teach. She worked on building trusting relationships with every interaction. She tried anything she could think of to engage teachers in conversation, hoping that would lead to working together. But working together rarely happened.

For three years, Maria truly didn't know what her job was. She knew what she needed to do with the students in her classes, but she had no idea who she was really "coaching" or what that should look like. She had left a job she enjoyed in a school community she loved, but now she felt physically and psychologically discon-nected from both students and teachers, and she felt like her job had to be more than this. Her annual evaluation was just a vague conversation, involving no form, no rubric, and no goal setting. Was she doing a good job? Finlay never seemed sure of how to answer that question, responding only with a "Well, of course." Having gone from the hyper-structured world of a classroom teacher to this nebulous portable purgatory, Maria felt uncertain, isolated, and sometimes like her position was perhaps a waste of money.

Maria wasn't the only one who sensed a problem. Other coaches around the district felt the same way, and leaders in the district knew that coaching was poorly defined and inconsistently imple-mented. So they decided to hire Jim to help them show coaches the best ways to engage teachers in coaching and the best process to use to bring about change for students. Maria and the other coaches were relieved and delighted. At last someone gave them a definition of coaching! At last they had a job description!

The coaches became part of Jim's research in developing the Impact Cycle process (Knight, 2017), and their work on coaching cycles as part of a multi-year writing project resulted in a jump from 10% to 90% of students meeting or exceeding the writing standards. The coaches became part of teams that developed a coach evaluation process and ways to measure the impact of the coaching program. Maria and her coaching colleagues now felt powerful, knowledgeable, and deeply engaged as coaches, and schools were changing as a result.

Still, trouble was not far away. Issues involving the board of education and the teacher union resulted in tense district-level conversations about what coaches do and what their role should be with teachers. Under increased pressure to justify the coaching positions, the coaches and Jim presented data to the board of education to make the case. Ironically, when the coaches had been largely unseen and underused, their presence had been less controversial, but now that they were starting to make a significant impact in schools, they became in some ways a lightning-rod that highlighted other historical problems with the school district's decision-making processes. In the end, the coaching positions were eliminated. Nearly every coach, including Maria, went back to a teaching role.

Sadly, Maria's story is an example of what we see in schools all the time. Instructional coaching is too often misunderstood, poorly supported, and short-lived. The research on the power of instructional coaching is incredibly compelling, yet programs still struggle to survive and thrive. This chapter provides important steps for how to support coaches and coaching programs to avoid endings like Maria's and instead ensure that instructional coaching becomes the valued, supported, and permanent part of teaching and learning that it should be.

Bring up the subject of district-wide change at any gathering of educators, and you're likely to hear the phrase "The pendulum swung again." Over the years, educators have become used to new people, new job positions, and new programs coming and going like the tides, and that sense of impermanence can lead to feelings of frustration and hopelessness about change in general.

Change doesn't become status quo on its own. Deep and lasting change requires advocates, dedication, and—above all—a plan to become a sustainable part of an organization. In this chapter, we examine how to address two of the primary pillars of the stability and expansion of instructional coaching: coach retention and coaching program sustainability.

The chapter focuses heavily on planning. The good news is that, if you structure your instructional coach hiring and evaluation practices as we describe in chapters 1-4, you have already done much of the groundwork for your plan. To keep good coaches coaching and good programs changing instruction for the better, this chapter assists you in predicting and preventing retention and sustainability problems so that coaches, teachers, and students can flourish.

To aid leaders in planning for retaining coaches and sustaining programs, we structure this chapter (and provide this checklist) around the most important facets of keeping coaching alive and well and working in schools.

RETAINING COACHES AND SUSTAINING PROGRAMS CHECKLISTS

PLAN FOR RETAINING COACHES

MAXIMIZE COACH ENGAGEMENT	✓
Collect data on the presence of a coach retention problem to use to inform the retention plan.	○
Identify opportunities for coach socialization with employees.	○
Identify systems of collaboration and support for coaches.	○
Identify practices around coach recruitment and role clarity.	○
Identify opportunities to support and enhance coach compensation and "rewards."	○
Identify issues around supervision of coaches that influence retention.	○
PROVIDE PROFESSIONAL LEARNING OPPORTUNITIES	✓
Ensure role clarity around what coaches do to aid in identified learning and training needs.	○
Assess coach needs for professional learning from the coaches' perspectives.	○
Assess coach needs for professional learning from the school or district perspective.	○
Develop a plan to provide ongoing professional learning experiences that are responsive to those identified needs.	○
Continuously evaluate the success of those professional learning experiences to determine future needs.	○
Encourage coaches to set their own goals for improvement and to identify their needs in hitting those goals. Provide resources to support those goals.	○

PLAN FOR SUSTAINING PROGRAMS CHECKLIST	✓
Consciously develop the professional culture.	○
Support the coaching champion.	○
Evaluate the coaching program continuously to make improvements.	○

Retaining Instructional Coaches

If we believe the reports of the educators we work with (and we do!), coaches are phenomenal employees and team members. Worldwide, we hear administrators and teachers rave about their coaches' knowledge, work ethic, and goodness. Districts invest a great deal in their coaches, especially in training on strategies and resources for the classroom. Coaches are, in our experience, overwhelmingly respected, beloved, and viewed as integral members of the school community. Why, then, do coaches leave those roles sometimes after just a few years?

The truth is, even though coaches are widely perceived as incredibly capable, accomplished professionals, they are also humans and employees with the same needs as anyone else. Understanding the elements of employee retention in general can provide a guide to retaining instructional coaches in particular. In this chapter, we examine the research on employee retention and connect it to coaching roles so that districts can develop plans to enhance coach retention specifically and not merely watch coach turnover or retention occur by accident.

Having a retention plan is important. According to the Society for Human Resource Management (SHRM), "Managing for employee retention involves strategic actions to keep employees motivated and focused so they elect to remain employed and fully productive for the benefit of the organization" (SHRM, 2021e, p. 1). Too often, SHRM says, focusing on retention is a task that managers put aside in favor of other pressures during their workday. But to set aside issues of job satisfaction means that potential workplace problems often go unaddressed, problems that could lead coaches (and others in the school) to become frustrated and consider other roles or other job environments.

School districts everywhere express concern about teacher or employee turnover. SHRM (2021e) clarifies that two types of turnover create job vacancies:

» Involuntary turnover, involving employees who are fired or laid off, and
» Voluntary turnover, involving employees who leave of their own volition.

Involuntary turnover may be unavoidable because of job performance issues or budget cuts. But voluntary turnover is often avoidable.

Voluntary turnover typically involves negative feelings about the job or the workplace that are preventable or could improve. "Studies have shown that employees typically follow four primary paths to turnover, each of which has different implications for an organization" (SHRM, 2021e, p. 4):

1. Employee dissatisfaction
2. Better alternatives
3. A planned change (e.g., a pregnancy, a move to a new home)
4. A negative experience (resignation that happens after a specific negative event or after dealing with a chronically negative situation)

When making the decision of whether to stay in a particular job or organization, employees form a mathematical equation in their minds: "Generally, an individual will stay with an organization if the pay, working conditions, developmental opportunities, etc., are equal to or greater than the contributions (e.g., time and effort) required of the employee" (SHRM, 2021e, p. 4). When considering the variables that form that equation, employees focus on five leading contributors (SHRM, 2021e):

1. Respectful treatment of all employees at all levels
2. Compensation/pay
3. Trust between employees and senior management
4. Job security
5. Opportunities to use their skills and abilities at work

Beyond these five contributors, SHRM (2021e) recommends additional focus on the following predictors of job satisfaction, some of which are directly tied to research on effective instructional coaching:

» Organizational commitment and job satisfaction
» Quality of the employee-supervisor relationship
» Role clarity
» Job design
» Workgroup cohesion

Yes, there they are again (albeit with different names): system support, role clarity, and humanizing partnership relationships. Three of the key elements of effective coaching programs are also key issues to focus on to retain instructional coaches.

To aid districts in developing retention plans for their instructional coaching positions, we have organized the research on retention and coaches into three major focus areas:

1. Emphasizing employee engagement
2. Developing strong coach-supervisor relationships
3. Providing professional learning opportunities

Using these three areas as a guide for a retention plan ensures that employers do not see instructional coaches as "superhuman," a perception that gives the false impression that coaches don't need support. Instead, employers need to see coaches as humans who, although highly skilled and capable, not only work to create positive environments for others but also need positive environments themselves.

EMPHASIZING EMPLOYEE ENGAGEMENT

The term *engagement* has never been more prevalent in education than it is today. Increasing understanding around the importance of engagement in student achievement and student behavior has made it one of our most frequent focus areas with coaches in the field. But despite all that educators have learned about engagement, engagement among the adults in schools is concerning (Money, 2015) and rarely receives attention on its own.

In a broad sense, *engagement* for employees involves "the level of an employee's commitment and connection to an organization" (SHRM, 2021d, p. 1). Paul Marciano (2010), author of *Carrots and Sticks Don't Work: Build a Culture of Employee Engagement with the Principles of Respect*, says, "Engaged employees are in the game for the sake of the game; they believe in the cause of the organization." One would hope for that level of engagement by all of the employees in a school, but in reality, that's not the case.

To determine whether coach engagement is an issue, examining the characteristics of engagement and disengagement can be helpful. SHRM (2021d) describes "engaged" employees as possessing these characteristics:

- » Optimistic
- » Team-oriented
- » Go above and beyond
- » Solution-oriented
- » Selfless
- » Show a passion for learning
- » Pass along credit but accept blame

Disengaged employees, on the other hand, display much different characteristics (SHRM, 2021d):

- » Pessimistic
- » Self-centered
- » High absenteeism
- » Negative attitude
- » Egocentric
- » Focus on monetary worth
- » Accept credit but pass along blame

Rarely have we seen instructional coaches whose traits fully match that second list, but for most employees, dissatisfaction isn't a case of "engaged all the time" versus "engaged not at all." Those behaviors can change by degrees according to the situation, and identifying trends toward more of the disengaged behaviors is likely more helpful than viewing these lists as all or none.

Likewise, Raymond Noe et al. (2008) describe a long-held human resources (HR) belief in the "theory of progression of withdrawal," the theory that "dissatisfied individuals enact a set of behaviors in succession to avoid their work situation" (p. 459). Work dissatisfaction doesn't occur overnight; rather, any of the following five areas can trigger it, build on it, and exacerbate it over time:

- » Working conditions
- » Personal disposition

» Tasks and roles

» Supervisors and coworkers

» Pay and benefits

As the employee becomes increasingly dissatisfied, behavior changes occur:

» Physical job withdrawal (the employee quits), or

» Psychological job withdrawal (although the employee remains physically on the job, their minds are elsewhere) (Noe et al., 2008)

The fact that job dissatisfaction is often progressive means that prevention and early intervention are key to employee retention.

What may be more complex than identifying disengaged employees is determining how to maximize their engaged colleagues. According to SHRM (2021e), "Engaged employees are satisfied with their jobs, enjoy their work and the organization, believe that their job is important, take pride in their company, and believe that their employer values their contributions" (p. 4).

How, then, do employers create the conditions for that depth of engagement? HR research identifies two important aspects of engagement that employers can develop:

1. Socialization opportunities
2. Systems of collaboration and support

SOCIALIZATION

SHRM's research (2021e) suggests that employees who "become embedded in their jobs and their communities" (p. 3) also have a higher level of engagement in their work. That sense of commitment to the work community means that leaving that job "would require severing or rearranging these social and value networks." Sharon remembers one of her former principals expressing her own beliefs in this area. If that principal discovered that any of the teachers in the building were dating each other, she would joke, "That's great! If they marry each other, they both stay in the school system." SHRM's research doesn't require a marital level of community commitment to improve engagement, but the overarching truth remains: Employees' attachment to the work community makes them more likely to stay.

Creating opportunities for employees to socialize and interact is important for work communities to develop and solidify. New teachers benefit from onboarding programs that allow them to meet each other and form supportive relationships; the same goes for new coaches. Interactions can range from ongoing formal learning experiences to initial and informal get-to-know-you activities (SHRM, 2021e) and can also include empowering coaches to create their own opportunities for community. Coaches routinely express to us how much they love getting together to discuss coaching, to develop Instructional Playbooks, and to share ideas about what they're working on with teachers, but at the same time, they communicate how rare such opportunities are. Providing coaches with the time and spaces to develop as communities benefits the coaches and their sense of connection to the job and the district.

SYSTEMS OF COLLABORATION AND SUPPORT

Earlier in the chapter, we listed SHRM's (2021e) five factors that are correlated with job satisfaction. Two of them, organizational commitment and workgroup cohesion, involve the employee's level of engagement both with the larger district and with work teams within the district. Support for both of these factors for coaches may involve

» providing mentors or other forms of support to coaches (see "Supporting the Coaching Champion" in this chapter),

» designing team-based projects that build community across the school and/or district,

» fostering team cohesiveness (e.g., building a partnership culture in schools, encouraging autonomy and ownership of team projects), and

» providing clear communication about the school and district's values and culture.

In providing as much positive professional collaboration as possible, the employer communicates a great deal about the value of employees, the focus on a partnership environment, and the belief that everyone benefits from support and from working with others. Focusing intentionally on the larger school or district culture in this way benefits not only coaches and their retention; it benefits everyone working in schools.

The Gallup organization's Q12 survey provides employers with questions that can help them to analyze engagement among instructional coaches or employees at large, such as whether employees feel that they have sufficient resources to do their work well, that they are supported by colleagues, that their opinions matter, that they are given opportunities to grow professionally, or that they have made personal connections at work (Gallup, 2021).

The questions ask employees to rate their *experience* of work and coworkers rather than rating their *job tasks* or the *behaviors* of their boss or coworkers specifically. Their responses can provide employers with a window into employees' perception of the work environment that can aid in planning opportunities for socialization and systems of collaboration and support.

Engagement is increasingly one of the deepest concerns that teachers have about their students. Wise school leaders focus just as much on the engagement of employees as they do on the engagement of children because more deeply engaged educators (teachers, coaches, counselors, administrators) create more engaging learning environments for students.

DEVELOPING STRONG COACH-SUPERVISOR RELATIONSHIPS

The employer-supervisor relationship is a central factor in employee job satisfaction (Noe et al., 2008; SHRM, 2021e). In instructional coaching, we know the critical role of system support (both district- and school-level leaders) in coaching success (Knight, 2022). Coaches' direct supervisors have enormous power in creating job environments in which they feel supported and able to do their very challenging work.

RECRUITMENT AND ROLE CLARITY

Recruitment practices that involve clear and realistic job descriptions aid in employee retention (SHRM, 2021e). The more information prospective job candidates have about the work they will be doing in their new role, the more likely they are to feel satisfied and fulfilled in that role. HR efforts to promote the role work best when they communicate clearly exactly what the role is.

Once on the job, the list of work tasks that coaches are expected to perform can expand unless constant attention is paid to how they spend their time during the work day and the negative impact of too many unrelated assignments has on deep coaching (Knight, 2022; see also chapter 2). SHRM's (2021e) research cites role clarity and job design as central to job satisfaction as well. This finding does not surprise us because we frequently see the frustration of coaches who are asked to be "all things to all people" in the school and feel that they do not have the time to do any of those tasks well.

Feeling stretched beyond the bounds of competence makes coaches feel as if they are having no impact.

Feeling like they are having no impact is an important impetus to leave the job. Supervisors who help to ensure role clarity are ensuring

- » that coaches have time for deep Impact Cycle work with teachers,
- » the deeper engagement of coaches in their work,
- » the retention of coaches in their roles, and
- » most important, the likelihood that coaching will positively affect student growth.

COMPENSATION AND REWARDS

SHRM (2021e) identifies compensation and pay as an important part of job satisfaction. This is a difficult issue in public schools because pay scales are determined by school boards and/or lawmakers in the various states, not by a coach's direct supervisor. As a result, district-level staff may have little or no say on the pay scale. Nonetheless, school and district leaders can direct attention in this area by zooming out from the concepts of "pay" and "rewards" to focus, instead, on communicating the coach's *value*. By consistently and clearly communicating the coach's value, supervisors add to the growth of the positive professional culture.

In Jim's book *Better Conversations* (Knight, 2016), one of the *Better Conversations* Habits for interacting more positively with others is "Be a Witness to the Good." *Witnessing the good* means communicating clearly the positive experiences we have of other people. This practice supports a more humanizing work environment and helps coaches to feel "seen" and valued for the good work they are doing. Being as specific as possible about the coach's actions is the most effective strategy for witnessing the good.

For example, saying "You're so organized" is not as effective in communicating value as saying, "The way you organized these materials for the stages of the strategy is so helpful. That will allow the teachers to have a visual aid as they learn them." Similarly, saying, "That session you facilitated today was great!" is not as effective in communicating value as "The feedback I'm hearing on today's session on equity in classroom management is that teachers feel like they have specific strategies to use to address that complex problem." Communicating these positive experiences (the valuable actions of the coach) aids in developing trust and rapport, and thus deeper employee engagement.

Communicating value can extend to issues of compensation as well, albeit indirectly. Because public education budgets are debated and decided in public forums, school and district leaders can be present at those forums to advocate for proposed pay increases for staff members and continued funding for instructional coaching programs. Seeing leaders actively support them in that regard can be a powerful demonstration of both empathy for employees and of the respect that leaders have for them. Making every effort to show how much employers value their coaches can aid in job retention for specific employees while also building community with the entire staff.

SUPERVISION

Not surprisingly, the degree to which employees feel that their employer is treating them fairly in terms of evaluation and in day-to-day supervision has a major impact on retention (SHRM, 2021e). Developing a strong and focused evaluation process for coaches (as we describe in chapter 2) is important in the perception of fairness, as is attention to day-to-day communications. Those coach-administrator meetings that we describe as part of the evaluation process are fertile ground for developing rapport and understanding between a coach and her supervisor. The more frequent, positive, and consistent that communication is among the two professionals, the less likely the coach is to feel misunderstood, maligned, or mistreated.

The tendency to view coaches as people who always "have it together" can foster a supervisor's perception that "They're fine; I don't need to check in with them." While mostly well-intended, such a perception can unintentionally send the relationship down a path of miscommunication and hard feelings. In the end, it's better for the employer to over-communicate with the coach than to under-communicate.

PROVIDING PROFESSIONAL LEARNING OPPORTUNITIES

All professionals want to feel that they do their jobs well and that they are growing in their roles. Lack of growth can have dire consequences for job satisfaction. "If employees are not given opportunities to continually update their skills, they are more inclined to leave" (SHRM, 2021e, p. 4). Creating professional learning opportunities for coaches that help to expand their capacity, encourage their growth, and offer them choices will allow coaches to feel that they are doing a good job and learning more about that job all the time.

Most successful coaching programs that we work with have a professional learning system in place. Alan Clardy (1997) emphasizes the importance of a systematic approach to professional learning, arguing that, for employees to perform best, leaders must

>> have a clear understanding of the tasks that employees must do,
>> base training needs on those tasks,
>> evaluate the success of training modules based on performance, and
>> adapt training to address areas identified on the evaluation.

Instructional coaches typically receive a great deal of "training" but not always with a systematic approach focused on what knowledge and skills they need to engage teachers more deeply in coaching.

To develop a professional learning model for coaches, school districts should assess coach needs and develop a structure in which to provide learning opportunities in those areas. Often, districts default to viewing "coaching PD" as involving solely the acquisition of new learning strategies that coaches will share with teachers. That focus on strategies neglects the crucial areas of how best to work with adults and implementing cycle-based coaching processes that are so important to coaching success. Surveying coaches on their needs and concerns for their coaching practice can help leaders determine the areas that most influence coaching and what additional learning and practice in those areas should look like. Ensuring funding and resources for that learning is another supervisory task that aids in long-term growth and, therefore, retention.

Moreover, in the context of those learning experiences, supervisors can encourage coaches to set goals for themselves and their coaching practice, whether inside or outside of the goals they set as part of their annual evaluation (see chapter 2). The benefits of reflection and goals are well established in terms of providing a sense of hope for future improvement (Lopez, 2013), and within the school setting, coaches need hope just as much as teachers do.

DEVELOPING A COACH RETENTION PLAN

To develop a plan to keep coaches feeling valued and effective in their jobs, employers can follow SHRM's (2021e) four-step process, which focuses heavily on the planning process, using data to inform decisions and steps to improve it, and reflection on what the needs are and what works best.

1. Determine whether coach turnover is a problem.
2. Establish a plan of action.
3. Implement a retention plan.
4. Evaluate the results to improve the plan.

Instructional coaches may well be some of the most motivated and engaged employees in a school district but that is no reason to ignore them and their very human needs. Time that employers spend on retention is time well spent indeed because it results in positively influencing all of the employees in the system.

Sustaining Instructional Coaching Programs

Atul Gawande (2011) says it best: "Coaching done well may be the most effective intervention designed for human performance" (p. 16). We seek to spread the word about the power of instructional coaching in everything we do. Beyond our work, coaching is a global phenomenon involving deep research and many thinkers, practitioners, professions, and resources. Coaching is everywhere. But beyond the standard characteristics of coaching, instructional coaching is also an education program, and that means that it is as subject to the whims of budget cuts, leadership changes, and government mandates as anything else in schools is.

Ian Palmer et al. (2009), in their book Managing Organizational Change: A Multiple Perspectives Approach, explain that, "One of the greatest challenges for those involved in managing change is to try to ensure that the change is not just a transitory phenomenon that 'flashes brightly' for a while before fading from the scene" (p. 355). According to the authors, a program's sustainability is not something to address once the program in place but something worth addressing before it is implemented: "Whether or not a change is sustained has a lot to do with the cumulative effect of actions during the change process, not just actions implemented after the change is in place" (Palmer et al., 2009, p. 359).

When planning for a sustainable coaching program, Palmer et al. (2009) recommend focusing on these actions:

- » Redesign roles (for coaching programs, this means ensuring role clarity in line with the vision for the program)
- » Redesign reward systems (for coaching programs, this means assigning "rewards" like positive attention and praise to tasks that match the program's vision)
- » Link hiring decisions to change objectives (for coaching programs, this means hiring coaches based on skills that directly connect to the coaching role [see chapter 4])
- » Act consistently with advocated actions (for coaching programs, this means focusing on actions that align with the program mission and not focusing time and attention on unrelated actions)
- » Encourage "voluntary actions of initiative" (for coaching programs, this means supporting coaches' and leaders'

autonomy in actions that support change [to avoid micromanaging the program])

» Measure progress (for coaching programs, this means gathering data on coaching goals and feedback from coaches and teachers to inform next steps)

» Celebrate "en route" (for coaching programs, this means acknowledging the work of coaches consistently and across their different tasks)

» Fine-tune as you go (for coaching programs, this means using data to "formatively assess" the data to make modifications as coaches go along, not just waiting for an annual program evaluation to make changes)

Note the importance of alignment and consistency among these action steps. For a program to be sustainable, its objectives, actions, and roles must be clear to everyone so that data regarding its effectiveness have a high degree of validity and trust. Alignment of all these elements ensures stronger implementation, which increases the likelihood of the program's success.

This book's focus on alignment among the standards for coaching (Appendix 1), the instructional coach's and the coaching program's evaluations (see chapters 2 and 3), and the job description and hiring practices for coaches (see chapter 4) all serve a purpose far beyond "fidelity": For instructional coaching programs to impact student growth, all of those program elements must support each other. Inconsistency in one area has a ripple effect in the other areas that does not serve students. Attention to this issue is critical for both program sustainability and for student impact.

To aid keeping a consistent focus on all aspects of the coaching program, we describe three areas that contribute greatly to program sustainability:

1. Consciously developing the professional culture
2. Supporting the coaching champion
3. Evaluating the program to make improvements

CONSCIOUSLY DEVELOPING THE PROFESSIONAL CULTURE

Ensuring that the district's larger professional culture is a positive and humanizing one lays the foundation for a coaching program founded on the Partnership Principles (Knight, 2007). Many thinkers have contributed to the research on what constitutes a happy and productive work environment.

Daniel Coyle (2018), in his book *The Culture Code: The Secrets of Highly Successful Groups*, says that, for successful work teams, "individual skills are not what matters. What matters is the inter-action" (p. xv). Because group interactions are the driver of team success, he describes effective teams as having the ability to do three things:

- » **SKILL 1**: Build Safety
- » **SKILL 2**: Share Vulnerability
- » **SKILL 3**: Establish Purpose

Leaders who create environments in which groups are able to let go of perceived status and territorial concerns are able to focus more deeply on their mission (or tasks) and, therefore, do a better job while also building relationships with each other.

Similarly, in his book *Six Secrets of Change: What the Best Leaders Do to Help Their Organizations Survive and Thrive* (2008), Michael Fullan presents six secrets that heavily emphasize the importance of a humanizing professional culture:

1. Love your employees
2. Connect peers with purpose
3. Capacity building prevails

4. Learning is the work
5. Transparency rules
6. Systems learn

Just as foundational communication skills are an important characteristic of instructional coaches (see chapter 4), they are important for leaders, too. Leaders who view leadership as a role that is "commanding" and involves wielding directives and oversight over their employees typically have employees who do not feel valued and who do not feel capable and skilled. (After all, their commander consistently tells them what their problems are and how to fix them.) Employees in those environments do not feel empowered and often don't work well in teams because they have little psychological safety to be anything other than "perfect."

By contrast, leaders who act in a more humanizing, servant-leadership vein have employees who feel safe in voicing concerns and taking risks, feel valued and empowered in making decisions, and trust their leaders more. Leaders who are willing to spend the time and effort in developing a professional culture like that will find benefits across the board—from employee performance, to employee retention, to program sustainability (SHRM, 2021d, 2021e).

SUPPORTING THE COACHING CHAMPION

Anyone who has been involved in school reform knows the crucial role that leadership changes play in program sustainability. Often, specific programs are viewed as a leader's pet project, and once that leader moves on to another role or another district, that project loses its funding. To ensure the success of coaching programs, both Jim and Joellen Killion (Killion et al., 2020) have long advocated for the role of a "coaching champion." The coaching champion may be a full-time position all on its own in a district with a large coaching program, or it could be part of the job description for a district-level administrator (assistant superintendent, director of professional learning, director of teaching and learning, etc.).

Killion and colleagues (2020) describe a coaching champion as a "vocal and proactive advocate for coaching who champions the work of coaches and broadcasts evidence of success of coaching" (p. 145). Effective coaching champions embody Palmer et al.'s (2009) description of strong change managers:

» **DIRECTOR** (ensures alignment of coaching with the program vision and objectives)
» **NAVIGATOR** (assists coaches and leaders in troubleshooting coaching concerns; sometimes act as intermediaries in issues that involve tension or confusion among school or district leaders and coaches)
» **CARETAKER** (handles barriers to coaching success)
» **COACH** (assists coaches in setting goals for improvement)
» **INTERPRETER** (fosters effective communication with various stakeholders about coaching)
» **NURTURER** (provides whatever the coaches and the coaching program need to thrive)

Having a designated coaching champion helps to insulate the coaching program from issues surrounding leadership change, at least to some extent. That dedicated coaching advocate can ensure that funding and resources for coaching continue regardless of who is in the various leadership roles, and also allows for consistency in messaging about what coaching is.

A particularly valuable role that a coaching champion plays is to serve as coach for the coaches themselves. Jim has long said that coaches should be the "most coached" people in the school, professionals who are continuously focused on their own improvement. To do that well and deeply means that they need a coach, too.

Coaching champions can assist coaches in setting goals and developing action plans for improving their coaching skills, for learning new instructional strategies, and for developing Instructional Playbooks and other important elements of excellent coaching practice.

EVALUATING THE PROGRAM TO MAKE IMPROVEMENTS

As we describe in detail in chapter 3, eveloping a system for continuous attention to each of these elements directly affects the short- and long-term success of instructional coaching. Regularly collecting data on the strength and impact of each of these elements can be used as part of evaluating the coaching program overall as well (as described in chapter 3).

Regularly gathering data to evaluate the instructional coaching program is key to its sustainability. Data on program success provide leaders with the ability to make improvements to the program based on those data, and data on student impact assist leaders in communicating the importance of maintaining coaching positions as part of the school budget.

Evaluating coaching programs also assists in transparency with stakeholders. With regular evaluation data, coaching champions and school and district leaders can communicate the benefits of coaching and also acknowledge areas for future growth.

ᆸᆸᆫ

Throughout this book, we have repeatedly emphasized four aspects of supporting coaches and coaching programs:

1. Careful planning for the coaching program
2. Role clarity for coaches
3. Alignment of all aspects of the coaching program
4. Consistent and clear communication about coaching with everyone

So much of these four elements may seem like common sense to educators, but, in the real world, the label of "common sense" can signal something that was "assumed to be happening already" (and wasn't) or something so obvious that it's "not worth spending more time on." Planning coaching programs, coaching evaluations, coaching hiring processes, and how to sustain coaches and coaching programs is worth the time it takes to do those things well. Creating job structures that align well with research on coaching and that also align well with evaluation structures and employee retention practices ensures that everyone involved with coaching knows coaching best practices and how those practices connect to student growth and to positive professional workplaces. As Killion and colleagues (2020) say, "When the structures to support coaching are in place, coaching is easier to sustain" (p. 145). When districts sustain research-based coaching, instructional coaches, teachers, and leaders all benefit, but students benefit the most.

 ## To Sum Up

Retaining instructional coaches requires an intentional focus on employee engagement, strong coach-supervisor relationships, professional learning opportunities for coaches, and development of a coach retention plan. Like all employees, instructional coaches deserve attention to their job satisfaction and development as professionals. Sustaining instructional coaching programs requires consciously developing the professional culture of the district or school, supporting the work of the coaching champion, and continuously evaluating the program to make improvements. Sustaining coaching programs does not happen by accident but requires a consistent focus on data to chart the path forward and on communication with stakeholders about coaching progress.

Making It Real

To make retaining coaches and sustaining programs real, begin the groundwork for developing a plan for retaining coaches. Survey coaches on the different aspects of job satisfaction, and seek guidance from HR professionals about how to approach the plan.

◷ Reflection Questions

What was most valuable in this chapter?

How do you currently address retention and sustainability issues for your instructional coaches and coaching program?

What specific issues regarding voluntary turnover of coaches concern you most?

Which types of data or evidence would you want to see as part of planning for improving retaining coaches and sustaining programs?

....

....

....

Do you have a designated coaching champion in the district whose
job it is to support coaches and coaching? If not, what could that
role look like in your context?

....

....

....

....

....

What resources would help you in developing a plan for retaining
coaches and sustaining coaching programs?

....

....

....

....

....

....

⊙ Going Deeper:
___

Further exploration of some of the workplace literature we mention in this chapter can be helpful in developing a vision around improving employee retention, including *The Culture Code* (Coyle, 2018), *The Six Secrets of Change* (Fullan, 2008), and the resources from the Gallup organization (2021). To more deeply explore sustaining instructional coaching programs, you may find help in Joellen Killion's *Assessing Impact* (2018), Killion et al.'s *Coaching Matters* (2020), and Jim's *Definitive Guide to Instructional Coaching* (Knight, 2022), which examine coaching concerns from the school and district level that can aid leaders in preventing the kind of program problems we examined in Maria's story at the start of this chapter.

REFERENCES

Campbell, J., & van Nieuwerburgh, C. (2018). *The leader's guide to coaching in schools*. Corwin.

Cappelli, P. (2019, April 29). *Viewpoint: Your approach to hiring is all wrong*. Retrieved from https://www.shrm.org/resourcesandtools/hr-topics/talent-acquisition/pages/viewpoint-your-approach-to-hiring-is-all-wrong.aspx

Clardy, A. (1997). *Studying your workforce*: Applied research methods and tools for the training and development practitioner. Sage.

Coyle, D. (2018). *The culture code: The secrets of highly successful groups*. Penguin Random House UK.

Danielson, C. (2007). *Enhancing professional practice: A framework for teaching* (2nd ed.). Association for Supervision and Curriculum Development.

Davenport, T. (2005). *Thinking for a living: How to get better performance and results from knowledge workers*. Harvard Business Review Press.

Eberhardt, J. L. (2019). *Biased: Uncovering the hidden prejudice that shapes what we see, think, and do*. Penguin.

Edmondson, A. C. (2019). *The fearless organization: Creating psychological safety in the workplace for learning, innovation, and growth.* Wiley.

Fleischer, C. H. (2018). *The SHRM essential guide to employment law.* Society for Human Resource Management.

Frazier, R. (2021). *The joy of coaching.* Corwin.

Fullan, M. (2008). *The six secrets of change: What the best leaders do to help their organizations survive and thrive.* Jossey-Bass.

Gallup. (2021). *The power of Gallup's Q^{12} employee engagement survey.* Retrieved from https://www.gallup.com/access/323333/q12-employee-engagement-survey.aspx

Gawande, A. (2011, September 26). *Personal best.* The New Yorker. Retrieved from https://www.newyorker.com/magazine/2011/10/03/personal-best

Grant, A. (Host). (2020a, April 20). *Reinventing the job interview* (No. 26) [Audio podcast episode]. In *Work Life.* https://podcasts.apple.com/us/podcast/reinventing-the-job-interview/id1346314086?i=1000472139819

Grant, A. (2021). *Think again: The power of knowing what you don't know.* Viking.

Guskey, T. R. (2000). *Evaluating professional development.* Corwin.

Instructional Coaching Group. (2020). *2019-2020 Katy ISD instructional coaching program audit report.* Author.

Killion, J. (2018). *Assessing impact: Evaluating professional learning.* Corwin.

Killion, J., Bryan, C., & Clifton, H. (2020). *Coaching matters* (2nd ed.). Learning Forward.

Kirkpatrick, J. D., & Kirkpatrick, W. K. (2016). *Kirkpatrick's four levels of training evaluation*. ATD Press.

Knight, J. (2007). *Instructional Coaching: A Partnership Approach to Improving Instruction*. Corwin.

Knight, J. (2011). *Unmistakable Impact*: A partnership approach for dramatically improving instruction. Corwin.

Knight, J. (2013). *High-Impact Instruction: A framework for great teaching*. Corwin.

Knight, J. (2014). *Focus on Teaching: Using video for High-Impact Instruction*. Corwin.

Knight, J. (2016). *Better Conversations: Coaching Ourselves and Each Other to Be More Credible, Caring, and Connected*. Corwin.

Knight, J. (2017). *The impact cycle: What instructional coaches should do to foster powerful improvements in teaching*. Corwin.

Knight, J. (2022). *The definitive guide to instructional coaching*: Seven factors for success. ASCD.

Knight, J., Cornett, J., Skrtic, T., Kennedy, M., Novosel, L., & Mitchell, B. (2010). *Understanding attributes of effective coaches*. Paper presented at the annual meeting of the American Educational Research Association, Denver, CO.

Knight, J., Hoffman, A., Harris, M., & Thomas, S. (2020). *The instructional playbook: The missing link for translating research into practice*. One Fine Bird Press.

Knight, R. (2021, March 8). *When to take a chance on an imperfect job candidate*. Harvard Business Review. Retrieved from https://hbr.org/2021/03/when-to-take-a-chance-on-an-imperfect-job-candidate

Lee, C. D. (2020, April 23). *Don't confuse feedback with a performance appraisal*. Retrieved from SHRM, www.shrm.org/resourcesandtools/hr-topics/people-managers/pages/dont-confuse-feedback-with-performance-appraisal.aspx.

Lloyd, J. (2009, July 13). *360-degree feedback is powerful leadership development tool*. Retrieved from https://www.shrm.org/resourcesandtools/hr-topics/organizational-and-employee-development/pages/360-degreefeedback.aspx

Lopez, S. J. (2013). *Making hope happen: Create the future you want for yourself and others*. Atria.

Marciano, P. L. (2010). *Carrots and sticks don't work: Build a culture of employee engagement with the principles of respect*. McGraw-Hill.

Money, J. (2015, January 20). Gallup: Majority of teachers "not" engaged" with their jobs. *Education Week*. Retrieved from https://www.edweek.org/technology/gallup-majority-of-teachers-not-engaged-with-their-jobs/2015/01

National Center for Education Statistics. (2021, May). *The condition of education: Executive summary*. https://nces.ed.gov/programs/coe/summary.asp

No Child Left Behind Act of 2001, Pub. L. No. 107-110 (2001). https://www2.ed.gov/nclb

Noe, R. A., Hollenbeck, J. R., Gerhart, B., & Wright, P. M. (2008). *Human resource management: Gaining a competitive advantage* (6th ed.). McGraw-Hill.

Onley, D. (2021, February 23). *These interview questions could get HR into trouble.* Retrieved from https://www.shrm.org/resourcesandtools/hr-topics/talent-acquisition/pages/interview-questions-hr-trouble.aspx

Palmer, I., Dunford, R., & Akin, G. (2009). *Managing organizational change: A multiple perspectives approach.* McGraw-Hill/Irwin.

Patton, E. (2018, May 8). *Want to really get to know your candidates? Interview for emotional intelligence.* Retrieved from https://www.shrm.org/resourcesandtools/hr-topics/talent-acquisition/pages/want-to-really-get-to-know-your-candidates-interview-for-emotional-intelligence.aspx

Pink, D. (2009). *Drive: The surprising truth about what motivates us.* Riverhead Books.

Prochaska, J. O., Norcross, J. C., & DiClemente, C. C. (1994). *Changing for good: A revolutionary six-stage program for overcoming bad habits and moving your life positively forward.* HarperCollins.

Rosenholtz, S. J. (1985, May). *Effective schools: Interpreting the evidence.* American Journal of Education, 93(3), 352-388. http://www.jstor.org/stable/1085385

Schein, E. (2009). *Helping: How to offer, give, and receive help.* Berret-Koehler Publishers.

Smart, G., & Street, R. (2008). *Who.* Ballantine Books.

Snyder, C. R. (2003). *The psychology of hope: You can get there from here*. Free Press.

Society for Human Resource Management. (2021a, February 23). *How to target passive job seekers*. Retrieved from https://www.shrm.org/resourcesandtools/tools-and-samples/how-to-guides/pages/how-to-target-passive-job-seekers.aspx

Society for Human Resource Management. (2021b, February 23). *Interviewing candidates for employment*. Retrieved from https://www.shrm.org/resourcesandtools/tools-and-samples/toolkits/pages/interviewingcandidatesforemployment.aspx

Society for Human Resource Management. (2021c, February 23). *Recruiting internally and externally*. Retrieved from https://www.shrm.org/resourcesandtools/tools-and-samples/toolkits/pages/recruitinginternallyandexternally.aspx

Society for Human Resource Management. (2021d, March 2). *Developing and sustaining employee engagement*. Retrieved from https://www.shrm.org/resourcesandtools/tools-and-samples/toolkits/pages/sustainingemployeeengagement.aspx

Society for Human Resource Management. (2021e, March 2). *Managing for employee retention*. Retrieved from https://www.shrm.org/ResourcesAndTools/tools-and-samples/toolkits/Pages/managingforemployeeretention.aspx

Stanier, M. B. (2016). *The coaching habit*. Box of Crayons Press.

Stone, D., & Heen, S. (2014). *Thanks for the feedback: The science and art of receiving feedback well*. Penguin.

Suzman, J. (2020). *Work: A deep history, from the stone age to the age of robots*. Penguin.

Taylor, S. (2011, July 12). *Assess pros and cons of 360-degree performance appraisal*. Retrieved from https://www.shrm.org/resourcesandtools/hr-topics/employee-relations/pages/360degreeperformance.aspx

Thomas, S. (2018a, December 13). Success factor 6: Leadership. *Radical Learners*. https://instructionalcoaching.com/success-factor-6-leadership

Thomas, S. (2018b, December 20). Success factor 7: System support. *Radical Learners*. https://instructionalcoaching.com/success-factor-7-system-support/

U. S. Department of Education. (November 2009). *Race to the top: Executive summary*. Author.

van Nieuwerburgh, C. (2017). *An introduction to coaching skills: A practical guide* (2nd ed.). Sage.

APPENDIX 1

Standards and Quality Indicators for Instructional Coaches

⎯⎯⎯

Modified from the ICG Coaching Certification program
(www.instructionalcoaching.com/certifications)

The coach demonstrates current, accomplished coaching practice around the **SEVEN SUCCESS FACTORS** for effective coaching programs (Knight, 2021).

STANDARD 1

PARTNERSHIP PRINCIPLES

No matter how much knowledge instructional coaches have, they will not be effective change leaders unless they understand the complexities of helping and working with adults. Instructional coaches demonstrate that they understand how to interact with adults in ways that do not engender resistance.

QUALITY INDICATOR 1.1

The coach uses a dialogical approach (Knight, 2017) to coaching in which the coach and teachers are partners who use their collective strengths to make powerful classroom changes for students.

QUALITY INDICATOR 1.2

The coach consistently embodies the Partnership Principles (Knight, 2011) in coaching interactions to build trusting relationships with teachers and school and system leaders.

STANDARD 2

THE IMPACT CYCLE

Instructional coaches effectively implement the Impact Cycle to partner with teachers in achieving their student-focused goals (Knight, 2017).

Identify

QUALITY INDICATOR 2.1

The coach partners with the teacher in obtaining a clear picture of current reality by using video, student interviews, student work, and/or observation data. [Current Reality]

QUALITY INDICATOR 2.2

The coach uses the Identify Questions with the teacher to set a measurable student-focused goal. [Goal]

QUALITY INDICATOR 2.3

The coach uses an Instructional Playbook to aid the teacher in choosing a high-impact teaching strategy to use to achieve the PEERS goal. [Strategy]

Learn

QUALITY INDICATOR 2.4

The coach uses a checklist to explain the chosen teaching strategy to the teacher and prompts the teacher to modify the strategy as the teacher wishes. [Checklists]

QUALITY INDICATOR 2.5

The coach models the strategy using a modeling approach that the teacher has chosen. [Modeling]

Improve

QUALITY INDICATOR 2.6

The coach begins every coaching conversation by asking the teacher about the teacher's most pressing concerns. [Confirm Direction]

QUALITY INDICATOR 2.7

The coach partners with the teacher in gathering and analyzing data on student progress toward the PEERS goal. [Review Progress]

QUALITY INDICATOR 2.8

The coach partners with the teacher in making modifications until students achieve the PEERS goal. [Invent Improvements]

QUALITY INDICATOR 2.9

The coach partners with the teacher in determining more long-term work on the goal as necessary or on future goals once the goal is met. [Plan Next Actions]

STANDARD 3
DATA

Instructional coaches partner with teachers to set PEERS goals and to monitor teachers' progress toward those goals, and that means that coaches must be able to gather and analyze data. (A description of the important data that coaches should gather and PEERS goals is included in Knight, 2017.)

QUALITY INDICATOR 3.1

The coach partners with the teacher in using video, student interviews, student work, and/or observation data to obtain a clear picture of current reality in the classroom in an area of teacher-identified need.

QUALITY INDICATOR 3.2

The coach partners with the teacher in determining the form of measurement and appropriate data tools for a PEERS goal and how to track progress over time.

QUALITY INDICATOR 3.3

The coach partners with the teacher in gathering and analyzing data on the goal until students meet the goal.

INSTRUCTIONAL PLAYBOOK

Instructional coaches use an Instructional Playbook to partner with teachers to choose a strategy to achieve their PEERS goals. (See Knight, 2017, and Knight et al., 2020, for examples of Instructional Playbooks.)

QUALITY INDICATOR 4.1

The coach creates, maintains, and periodically updates an Instructional Playbook tailored to the coaching audience that contains a selection of thoroughly vetted high-impact strategy choices for teachers to use to achieve their PEERS goals.

QUALITY INDICATOR 4.2

The coach uses the Instructional Playbook during the Identify Questions conversation to offer strategy choices to teachers.

QUALITY INDICATOR 4.3

The Instructional Playbook contains a Table of Contents of instructional strategies, a One-Page Summary for each strategy in the Table of Contents, sufficient checklists for each strategy, and an explanation of the coaching audience and how the playbook meets their current needs.

STANDARD 5

COMMUNICATION HABITS AND SKILLS

Because coaching involves communication, instructional coaches continually engage in improving their communication skills and in communicating about coaching with all school stakeholders to build a collaborative school culture.

QUALITY INDICATOR 5.1

The coach communicates with teachers in a spirit of partnership as evidenced by use of the *Better Conversations* Habits (Demonstrating Empathy, Listening, Fostering Dialogue, Asking Better Questions, Making Emotional Connections, Being a Witness to the Good, Finding Common Ground, Controlling Toxic Emotions, Redirecting Toxic Conversations, and Building Trust) as appropriate in coaching conversations (Knight, 2016).

QUALITY INDICATOR 5.2

The coach communicates about the coaching role, the coaching approach, and the coaching process regularly with school and system administrators and teachers to foster a collaborative school culture.

STANDARD 6
LEADERSHIP

Instructional coaches are emotionally intelligent, responsive to teachers, embody a stewardship approach during coaching, are ambitious for students, organized, and reliable (see Knight, 2016, chapter 9). In other words, effective coaches are effective leaders.

QUALITY INDICATOR 6.1

The coach has built trusting relationships with teachers that have resulted in many teachers choosing to work with the coach in Impact Cycles.

QUALITY INDICATOR 6.2

The coach has an exceptional level of instructional expertise and shares that knowledge with teachers as appropriate but does so dialogically as a partner, not as an "expert" or as an evaluator.

SYSTEM SUPPORT

Instructional coaches flourish in systems that support them. When district leaders and, in particular, principals, support instructional coaches, effective coaches succeed. However, when support does not exist, effective coaches may have little or no impact (Knight, 2011).

QUALITY INDICATOR 7.1

The coach has worked with school and/or district leadership to clarify the coach's role in the school, to clarify how the coach should spend the time during the workday (with the majority of time spent working with teachers in Impact Cycles), to clarify the boundaries of confidentiality in coaching, and to communicate these policies and practices to teachers.

QUALITY INDICATOR 7.2

The coach communicates regularly with school and/or district leadership to ensure that everyone who supports coaching views it with the same theoretical perspective and to address issues concerning the coaching role.

APPENDIX 2

Rubric for Instructional Coaches

––––––

Adapted from the ICG Coaching Certification program (www.instructionalcoaching.com/certifications)

The coach demonstrates current, accomplished coaching practice around the **SEVEN SUCCESS FACTORS** for effective coaching programs (Knight, 2021).

PARTNERSHIP PRINCIPLES

No matter how much knowledge instructional coaches have, they will not be effective change leaders unless they understand the complexities of helping and working with adults. Instructional coaches demonstrate that they understand how to interact with adults in ways that do not engender resistance.

QUALITY INDICATOR 1.1

The coach uses a dialogical approach (Knight, 2017) to coaching, in which the coach and teachers are partners who use their collective strengths to make powerful classroom changes for students.

QUALITY INDICATOR 1.2

The coach consistently embodies the Partnership Principles (Knight, 2011) in coaching interactions to build trusting relationships with teachers and school and system leaders.

SCORE OF 1	SCORE OF 2	SCORE OF 3	SCORE OF 4
the coach does not work with teachers as a partner	the coach unevenly works with teachers as a partner	the coach consistently works with teachers as a partner	the coach extensively works with teachers as a partner
the coach minimally uses a dialogical approach to coaching (Equality, Choice, Voice, and Reflection and Demonstrating Empathy, Listening, and Asking Better Questions)	the coach inconsistently uses a dialogical approach to coaching (Equality, Choice, Voice, and Reflection and Demonstrating Empathy, Listening, and Asking Better Questions)	the coach often uses a dialogical approach to coaching (Equality, Choice, Voice, and Reflection and Demonstrating Empathy, Listening, and Asking Better Questions)	the coach extensively uses a dialogical approach to coaching (Equality, Choice, Voice, and Reflection and Demonstrating Empathy, Listening, and Asking Better Questions)
the coach does not share expertise with the teacher positioned as the decision-maker	the coach inconsistently shares expertise with the teacher positioned as the decision-maker	the coach often shares expertise with the teacher positioned as the decision-maker	the coach effectively shares expertise with the teacher positioned as the decision-maker

the coach does not work with school and/ or district leadership to clarify the theoretical basis of dialogical coaching so that the coach and leaders agree on what "instructional coaching" is	the coach infrequently works with school and/ or district leadership to clarify the theoretical basis of dialogical coaching so that the coach and leaders agree on what "instructional coaching" is	the coach consistently works with school and/ or district leadership to clarify the theoretical basis of dialogical coaching so that the coach and leaders agree onwhat "instructional coaching" is	the coach extensively works with school and/ or district leadership to clarify the theoretical basis of dialogical coaching so that the coach and leaders agree on what "instructional coaching" is

STANDARD 2

THE IMPACT CYCLE

Instructional coaches effectively implement the Impact Cycle to partner with teachers in achieving their student-focused goals (Knight, 2017).

Identify

QUALITY INDICATOR 2.1

The coach partners with the teacher in obtaining a clear picture of current reality by using video, student interviews, student work, and/or observation data. [Current Reality]

QUALITY INDICATOR 2.2

The coach uses the Identify Questions with the teacher to set a measurable student-focused goal. [Goal]

QUALITY INDICATOR 2.3

The coach uses an Instructional Playbook to aid the teacher in choosing a high-impact teaching strategy to use to achieve the PEERS goal. [Strategy]

SCORE OF 1	SCORE OF 2	SCORE OF 3	SCORE OF 4
the coach ineffectively uses the Identify Questions to set a goal for students	the coach partially or vaguely uses the Identify Questions to set a goal for students	the coach effectively uses the Identify Questions to set a goal for students	the coach insightfully uses the Identify Questions to set a PEERS goal for students
the teacher does not select the teaching strategy to achieve the goal and/or is not provided with an Instructional Playbook to use to choose a strategy	the teacher selects the teaching strategy to achieve the goal, but an Instructional Playbook is not used to choose a strategy	the teacher selects the teaching strategy to achieve the goal and is provided with an appropriate Instructional Playbook to use to choose a strategy	the teacher selects the teaching strategy to achieve the goal by using a complete Instructional Playbook to choose a strategy

Learn

QUALITY INDICATOR 2.4

The coach uses a checklist to explain the chosen teaching strategy to the teacher and prompts the teacher to modify the strategy as the teacher wishes. [Checklists]

QUALITY INDICATOR 2.5

The coach models the strategy using a modeling approach that the teacher has chosen. [Modeling]

SCORE OF 1	SCORE OF 2	SCORE OF 3	SCORE OF 4
the coach does not use a checklist to explain the teaching strategy that the teacher has chosen to achieve the PEERS goal	the coach minimally uses a checklist to explain the teaching strategy that the teacher has chosen to achieve the PEERS goal	the coach consistently uses a checklist to explain the teaching strategy that the teacher has chosen to achieve the PEERS goal	the coach thoroughly and dialogically uses a checklist to explain the teaching strategy that the teacher has chosen to achieve the PEERS goal
the coach does not encourage the teacher to modify the checklist according to student needs	the coach provides little encouragement for the teacher to modify the checklist according to student needs	the coach encourages the teacher to modify the checklist according to student needs	the coach significantly encourages the teacher to modify the checklist according to student needs

the coach does not model the teaching strategy that the teacher chose to achieve the PEERS goal and/or does not provide the teacher with the six modeling options from which to choose	the coach minimally models the teaching strategy that the teacher chose to achieve the PEERS goal and/or provides the teacher with limited modeling options from which to choose	the coach effectively models the teaching strategy that the teacher chose to achieve the PEERS goal and provides the teacher with the six modeling options from which to choose	the coach thoroughly models the teaching strategy that the teacher chose to achieve the PEERS goal, including providing the teacher with the six modeling options from which to choose

Improve

QUALITY INDICATOR 2.6

The coach begins every coaching conversation by asking the teacher about the teacher's most pressing concerns. [Confirm Direction]

QUALITY INDICATOR 2.7

The coach partners with the teacher in gathering and analyzing data on student progress toward the PEERS goal. [Review Progress]

QUALITY INDICATOR 2.8

The coach partners with the teacher in making modifications until students achieve the PEERS goal. [Invent Improvements]

QUALITY INDICATOR 2.9

The coach partners with the teacher in determining more long-term work on the goal as necessary or on future goals once the goal is met. [Plan Next Actions]

SCORE OF 1	SCORE OF 2	SCORE OF 3	SCORE OF 4
the coach never begins coaching conversations by asking the teacher about the teacher's most pressing concerns [Confirm Direction]	the coach sometimes begins coaching conversations by asking the teacher about the teacher's most pressing concerns [Confirm Direction]	the coach often begins coaching conversations by asking the teacher about the teacher's most pressing concerns [Confirm Direction]	the coach always begins coaching conversation by asking the teacher about the teacher's most pressing concerns [Confirm Direction]
the coach does not assist the teacher in gathering and analyzing data on student progress toward the goal [Review Progress]	the coach minimally assists the teacher in gathering and analyzing data on student progress toward the goal [Review Progress]	the coach effectively assists the teacher in gathering and analyzing data on student progress toward the goal [Review Progress]	the coach extensively supports the teacher in gathering and analyzing data on student progress toward the goal [Review Progress]
the coach does not assist the teacher in making modifications until students meet the goal [Invent Improvements]	the coach minimally assists the teacher in making modifications until students meet the goal [Invent Improvements]	the coach effectively assists the teacher in making modifications until students meet the goal [Invent Improvements]	the coach extensively supports the teacher in making modifications until students meet the goal [Invent Improvements]
the coach does not assist the teacher in determining more long-term work on the goal as necessary or on future goals once the goal is met [Plan Next Actions]	the coach minimally assists the teacher in determining more long-term work on the goal as necessary or on future goals once the goal is met [Plan Next Actions]	the coach effectively assists the teacher in determining more long-term work on the goal as necessary or on future goals once the goal is met [Plan Next Actions]	the coach extensively supports the teacher in determining more long-term work on the goal as necessary or on future goals once the goal is met [Plan Next Actions]

STANDARD 3

DATA

Instructional coaches partner with teachers to set PEERS goals and to monitor teachers' progress toward those goals, and that means that coaches must be able to gather and analyze data. (A description of the important data that coaches should gather and PEERS goals is included in Knight, 2017.)

QUALITY INDICATOR 3.1

The coach partners with the teacher in using video, student interviews, student work, and/or observation data to obtain a clear picture of current reality in the classroom in an area of teacher-identified need.

The coach partners with the teacher in determining the form of measurement and appropriate data tools for a PEERS goal and how to track progress over time.

QUALITY INDICATOR 3.3

The coach partners with the teacher in gathering and analyzing data on the goal until students meet the goal.

SCORE OF 1	SCORE OF 2	SCORE OF 3	SCORE OF 4
the coach does not analyze or does not use appropriate data (classroom video, student interviews, student work, and/or coach observation data) to help the teacher get a clear picture of current reality and to choose a data-gathering process for the PEERS goal	the coach unevenly analyzes and/or uses appropriate data (classroom video, student interviews, student work, and/or coach observation data) to help the teacher get a clear picture of current reality and to choose a data-gathering process for the PEERS goal	the coach often analyzes and/or uses appropriate data (classroom video, student interviews, student work, and/or coach observation data) to help the teacher get a clear picture of current reality and to choose a data-gathering process for the PEERS goal	the coach extensively and insightfully analyzes and/or uses appropriate data (classroom video, student interviews, student work, and/or coach observation data) to help the teacher get a clear picture of current reality and to choose a data-gathering process for the PEERS goal
the coach does not use appropriate data to help the teacher get a clear picture of current reality	the coach minimally uses appropriate data to help the teacher get a clear picture of current reality	the coach effectively uses appropriate data to help the teacher get a clear picture of current reality	the coach extensively uses appropriate data to help the teacher get a clear picture of current reality
the coach does not help the teacher choose a data-gathering process for the PEERS goal	the coach minimally assists the teacher choose a data-gathering process for the PEERS goal	the coach assists the teacher in choosing a data-gathering process for the PEERS goal	the coach significantly assists the teacher in choosing a data-gathering process for the PEERS goal

STANDARD 4

INSTRUCTIONAL PLAYBOOK

Instructional coaches use an Instructional Playbook to partner with teachers to choose a strategy to achieve their PEERS goals. (See Knight, 2017, and Knight et al., 2020, for examples of Instructional Playbooks.)

QUALITY INDICATOR 4.1

The coach creates, maintains, and periodically updates an Instructional Playbook tailored to the coaching audience that contains a selection of thoroughly vetted high-impact strategy choices for teachers to use to achieve their PEERS goals.

QUALITY INDICATOR 4.2

The coach uses the Instructional Playbook during the Identify Questions conversation to offer strategy choices to teachers.

QUALITY INDICATOR 4.3

The coach's playbook contains a Table of Contents of instructional strategies, a One-Page Summary for each strategy In the Table of Contents, sufficient checklists for each strategy, and an explanation of the coaching audience and how the playbook meets their current needs.

SCORE OF 1	SCORE OF 2	SCORE OF 3	SCORE OF 4
the teacher does not select the teaching strategy to achieve the goal and/or is not provided with an Instructional Playbook to use to choose a strategy	the teacher selects the teaching strategy to achieve the goal, but an Instructional Playbook is not used to choose a strategy	the teacher selects the teaching strategy to achieve the goal and is provided with an appropriate Instructional Playbook to use for that task	the teacher selects the teaching strategy to achieve the goal by using a complete Instructional Playbook
the coach does not use an Instructional Playbook	the Instructional Playbook is incomplete and/or not clearly tied to the needs of the coaching audience	the Instructional Playbook is complete and minimally meets the needs of the coaching audience	the Instructional Playbook is complete and thoroughly meets the needs of the coaching audience

STANDARD 5
COMMUNICATION HABITS AND SKILLS

Because coaching involves communication, instructional coaches continually engage in improving their communication skills and in communicating about coaching with all school stakeholders to build a collaborative school culture.

The coach communicates with teachers in a spirit of partnership as evidenced by the use of the *Better Conversations* Habits (Demonstrating Empathy, Listening, Fostering Dialogue, Asking Better Questions, Making Emotional Connections, Being a Witness to the Good, Finding Common Ground, Controlling Toxic Emotions, Redirecting Toxic Conversations, and Building Trust) as appropriate in coaching conversations (Knight, 2016).

The coach communicates about the coaching role, the coaching approach, and the coaching process regularly with school and system administrators and teachers to foster a collaborative school culture.

COACHING APPROACH			
the coach does not use a dialogical approach to coaching (Equality, Choice, Voice, and Reflection and Demonstrating Empathy, Listening, and Asking Better Questions)	the coach inconsistently uses a dialogical approach to coaching (Equality, Choice, Voice, and Reflection and Demonstrating Empathy, Listening, and Asking Better Questions)	the coach often uses a dialogical approach to coaching (Equality, Choice, Voice, and Reflection and Demonstrating Empathy, Listening, and Asking Better Questions)	the coach extensively uses a dialogical approach to coaching (Equality, Choice, Voice, and Reflection and Demonstrating Empathy, Listening, and Asking Better Questions)
the coach does not share expertise with the teacher positioned as the decision-maker	the coach minimally shares expertise with the teacher positioned as the decision-maker	the coach consistently shares expertise with the teacher positioned as the decision-maker	the coach effectively shares expertise with the teacher and clearly positions the teacher as the decision-maker

COMMUNICATION			
the coach does not communicate about the coaching role with school and system administrators and teachers	the coach minimally communicates about the coaching role with school and system administrators and teachers	the coach consistently communicates about the coaching role with school and system administrators and teachers	the coach extensively communicates about the coaching role with school and system administrators and teachers

the coach does not communicate about the coaching approach with school and system administrators and teachers	the coach minimally communicates about the coaching approach with school and system administrators and teachers	the coach consistently communicates about the coaching approach regularly with school and system administrators and teachers	the coach extensively communicates about the coaching approach regularly with school and system administrators and teachers
the coach does not communicate about the coaching process with school and system administrators and teachers	the coach minimally communicates about the coaching process with school and system administrators and teachers	the coach consistently communicates about the coaching process regularly with school and system administrators and teachers	the coach extensively communicates about the coaching process regularly with school and system administrators and teachers
the coach does not help foster a collaborative school culture	the coach minimally fosters a collaborative school culture	the coach consistently fosters a collaborative school culture	the coach significantly fosters a collaborative school culture

STANDARD 6

LEADERSHIP

Instructional coaches are emotionally intelligent, responsive to teachers, embody a stewardship approach during coaching, are ambitious for students, organized, and reliable (see Knight, 2016, chapter 9). In other words, effective coaches are effective leaders.

QUALITY INDICATOR 6.1

The coach has built trusting relationships with teachers that have resulted in many teachers choosing to work with the coach in Impact Cycles.

QUALITY INDICATOR 6.2

The coach has an exceptional level of instructional expertise and shares that knowledge with teachers as appropriate but does so dialogically as a partner, not as an "expert" or as an evaluator.

SCORE OF 1	SCORE OF 2	SCORE OF 3	SCORE OF 4
few teachers and/or an inconsistent number of teachers voluntarily choose to work with the coach	a small but consistent number of teachers voluntarily choose to work with the coach	an appropriate and growing number of teachers voluntarily choose to work with the coach	a significant and growing number of teachers voluntarily choose to work with the coach
the coach does not interact with teachers and leaders as a partner	the coach inconsistently interacts with teachers and leaders as a partner and not as an "expert"	the coach consistently interacts with teachers and leaders as a partner and not as an "expert"	the coach extensively interacts with teachers and leaders as a partner and not as an "expert"

STANDARD 7

SYSTEM SUPPORT

Instructional coaches flourish in systems that support them. When district leaders and, in particular, principals, support instructional coaches, effective coaches succeed. However, when support does not exist, effective coaches may have little or no impact (Knight, 2011).

QUALITY INDICATOR 7.1

The coach has worked with school and/or district leadership to clarify the coach's role in the school, to clarify how the coach should spend the time during the workday (with the majority of time spent working with teachers in Impact Cycles), to clarify the boundaries of confidentiality in coaching, and to communicate these policies and practices to teachers.

QUALITY INDICATOR 7.2

The coach communicates regularly with school and/or district leadership to ensure that everyone who supports coaching views it with the same theoretical perspective and to address issues concerning the coaching role.

SCORE OF 1	SCORE OF 2	SCORE OF 3	SCORE OF 4
COMMUNICATION			
the coach does not communicate about the coaching role regularly with school and system administrators and teachers	the coach minimally communicates about the coaching role with school and system administrators and teachers	the coach consistently communicates about the coaching role with school and system administrators and teachers	the coach extensively communicates about the coaching role with school and system administrators and teachers
the coach does not communicate about the coaching approach regularly with school and system administrators and teachers	the coach minimally communicates about the coaching approach with school and system administrators and teachers	the coach consistently communicates about the coaching approach with school and system administrators and teachers	the coach extensively communicates about the coaching approach with school and system administrators and teachers
the coach does not communicate about the coaching process regularly with school and system administrators and teachers	the coach minimally communicates about the coaching process with school and system administrators and teachers	the coach consistently communicates about the coaching process with school and system administrators and teachers	the coach extensively communicates about the coaching process with school and system administrators and teachers
the coach does not help foster a collaborative school culture	the coach minimally fosters a collaborative school culture	the coach consistently fosters a collaborative school culture	the coach significantly fosters a collaborative school culture

SCORE OF 1	SCORE OF 2	SCORE OF 3	SCORE OF 4
ROLE CLARITY / TIME			
the coach does not work with school and/or district leadership to clarify the coach's role within the school	the coach minimally works with school and/or district leadership to clarify the coach's role within the school	the coach consistently works with school and/or district leadership to clarify the coach's role within the school	the coach extensively works with school and/or district leadership to clarify the coach's role within the school
the coach does not work with school and/or district leadership to clarify how the coach should spend the time during the workday	the coach minimally works with school and/or district leadership to clarify how the coach should spend the time during the workday	the coach consistently works with schooWl and/or district leadership to clarify how the coach should spend the time during the workday	the coach extensively works with school and/or district leadership to clarify how the coach should spend the time during the workday
the coach spends 0-25% of work time in Impact Cycles with teachers	the coach spends 26-45% of work time in Impact Cycles with teachers	the coach spends 46-59% of work time in Impact Cycles with teachers	the coach spends 60-100% of work time in Impact Cycles with teachers

SCORE OF 1	SCORE OF 2	SCORE OF 3	SCORE OF 4
CONFIDENTIALITY			
the coach does not work with school and/or district leadership to clarify the boundaries of confidentiality in coaching	the coach infrequently works with school and/or district leadership to clarify the boundaries of confidentiality in coaching	the coach consistently works with school and/or district leadership to clarify the boundaries of confidentiality in coaching	the coach extensively works with school and district leadership to clarify the boundaries of confidentiality in coaching
the coach does not work with school and/or district leadership to clarify how to communicate confidentiality policies and practices to teachers	the coach infrequently works with school and/or district leadership to clarify how to communicate confidentiality policies and practices to teachers	the coach consistently works with school and/or district leadership to clarify how to communicate confidentiality policies and practices to teachers	the coach extensively works with school and district leadership clarify how to communicate confidentitality policies and practices to teachers

SCORE OF 1	SCORE OF 2	SCORE OF 3	SCORE OF 4
PARTNERSHIP APPROACH			
the coach does not work with school and/or district leadership to clarify the theoretical basis of dialogical coaching so that the coach and leaders agree on what "instructional coaching" is	the coach infrequently works with school and/or district leadership to clarify the theoretical basis of dialogical coaching so that the coach and leaders agree on what "instructional coaching" is	the coach consistently works with school and/or district leadership to clarify the theoretical basis of dialogical coaching so that the coach and leaders agree on what "instructional coaching" is	the coach extensively works with school and/or district leadership to clarify the theoretical basis of dialogical coaching so that the coach and leaders agree on what "instructional coaching" is
the coach does not use a partnership approach in which the coach shares expertise dialogically	the coach unevely uses a partnership approach in which the coach shares expertise dislogically	the coach consistently uses a partnership approach in which the coach shares expertise dislogically	the coach thoroughly embodies a partnership approach in which the coach shares expertise dislogically

For the Teacher, Coaching Feedback Form

The heart of instructional coaching is professional improvement that serves the best interests of students. This form describes key aspects of the role that research demonstrates have the greatest impact on students and schools.

1. The coach partnered with me to gain a clear picture of reality in the classroom by analyzing one or more of the following forms of data: videorecording, student data, student interviews, and collecting classroom data at my request. (Indicators 1.1 and 3.1)

- O Always
- O Frequently
- O Sometimes
- O Rarely or Never

2. The coach partnered with me to identify a clear, powerful, measurable, student-focused goal that was emotionally compelling for me. (Indicators 1.2 and 3.2)

- O Always
- O Frequently
- O Sometimes
- O Rarely or Never

3. The coach used the instructional playbook with high-impact strategies to offer me choices in strategies to use to hit my student-focused goal. (Indicator 1.3)

- O Always
- O Frequently
- O Sometimes
- O Rarely or Never

4. The coach used checklists to describe clearly the teaching strategy that I chose to implement to hit my student-focused goal. (Indicator 1.4)

- O Always
- O Frequently

○ Sometimes

○ Rarely or Never

5. The coach encouraged me to modify the strategies I used for my student-focused goals to meet student needs. (Indicator 1.4)

○ Always

○ Frequently

○ Sometimes

○ Rarely or Never

6. The coach modeled teaching strategies that assisted me with understanding the strategy to meet my student-focused goals in one or more of the following ways at my request: (Indicator 1.5)

Teaching in my classroom

Co-teaching in my classroom

Before or after class (with no students in the room)

Observing another teacher's classroom (with the coach)

Observing another teacher's classroom (without the coach

Providing me with video of a teacher using the strategy

○ Yes

○ No

7. The coach partnered with me to problem solve and analyze goal progress until the goal was met: (Indicators 1.6, 1.7, 1.8, 1.9, and 3.3)

○ Always

○ Frequently

○ Sometimes

○ Rarely or Never

9. The coach treated me as a partner and encouraged dialogue over giving advice or directives. (Indicators 4.1 and 4.2)

- ○ Always
- ○ Frequently
- ○ Sometimes
- ○ Rarely or Never

10. The coach positioned me as the primary decision-maker in the Impact Cycle. (Indicators 5.1 and 5.2)

- ○ Always
- ○ Frequently
- ○ Sometimes
- ○ Rarely or Never

10. The coach has built a trusting relationship with me that has led me to be willing to work with the coach in Impact Cycles. (Indicator 6.1)

- ○ Always
- ○ Rarely or Never

11. The coach shared instructional knowledge with me dialogically as a partner and not as an "expert" or as an evaluator. (Indicator 6.2)

- ○ Always
- ○ Frequently
- ○ Sometimes
- ○ Rarely or Never

12. The coach made time to work with me on my goal for students. (Indicators 7.1 and 7.2)

- ○ Always
- ○ Frequently
- ○ Sometimes
- ○ Rarely or Never

13. The coach kept my Impact Cycle experience confidential. (Indicators 7.1 and 7.2)

○   Yes

○   No

For the Instructional Coach, Self-Evaluation Form

———

The heart of instructional coaching is professional improvement that serves the best interests of students. This form describes key aspects of the role that research demonstrates have the greatest impact on students and schools.

1. I partner with teachers to gain a clear picture of reality in the classroom by analyzing one or more of the following forms of data: video recording, student data, student interviews, and collecting classroom data at the request of the teacher. (Indicators 1.1 and 3.1)

   - O Always
   - O Frequently
   - O Sometimes
   - O Rarely or Never

2. I partner with teachers to identify clear, powerful, measurable, student-focused goals that are emotionally compelling for the teacher. (Indicators 1.2 and 3.2)

   - O Always
   - O Frequently
   - O Sometimes
   - O Rarely or Never

3. I use an Instructional Playbook with high-impact strategies to offer teachers choices in selecting strategies to use to hit their student-focused goals. (Indicator 1.3)

   - O Always
   - O Frequently
   - O Sometimes
   - O Rarely or Never

4. I use checklists to describe clearly the teaching strategies that teachers choose to implement to hit their student-focused goals. (Indicator 1.4)

   - O Always
   - O Frequently

○   Sometimes

○   Rarely or Never

5.   I encourage teachers to modify the strategies they use for their student-focused goals to meet student needs. (Indicator 1.4)

○   Always

○   Frequently

○   Sometimes

○   Rarely or Never

6.   I model teaching strategies that assist teachers with understanding the strategy to meet their student-focused goals in one or more of the following ways: (Indicator 1.5)

Teaching in the teacher's classroom

Co-teaching in the teacher's classroom

Before or after class (with no students in the room)

Observing another teacher's classroom (with the coach)

Observing another teacher's classroom (without the coach)

Providing the teacher with video of a teacher using the strategy

○   Always

○   Frequently

○   Sometimes

○   Rarely or Never

7.   I partner with teachers to problem solve and analyze goal progress until the goal is met. (Indicators 1.6, 1.7, 1.8, 1.9, and 3.3)

○   Always

○   Frequently

○   Sometimes

○   Rarely or Never

8. I treat all educators as partners and encourage dialogue over giving advice or directives. (Indicators 4.1 and 4.2)

- ○ Always
- ○ Frequently
- ○ Sometimes
- ○ Rarely or Never

9. I understand the complexities of working with adults and position teachers as the primary decision-makers in the Impact Cycle. (Indicators 5.1 and 5.2)

- ○ Always
- ○ Frequently
- ○ Sometimes
- ○ Rarely or Never

10. I have built trusting relationships with teachers that have led an increased number of teachers to be willing to work with me in Impact Cycles. (Indicator 6.1)

- ○ Always
- ○ Frequently
- ○ Sometimes
- ○ Rarely or Never

11. I share my instructional knowledge dialogically as a partner and not as an "expert" or as an evaluator. (Indicator 6.2)

- ○ Always
- ○ Frequently
- ○ Sometimes
- ○ Rarely or Never

12. I spend the following amount of my time on coaching cycles in which teachers set their own goals for students (Indicators 7.1 and 7.2)

- ○ 70% or more
- ○ 50-69%
- ○ 30-49%
- ○ less than 30%

13. I communicate regularly with school and system leadership about coaching while maintaining confidentiality. (Indicators 7.1 and 7.2)

- ○ Weekly
- ○ Monthly
- ○ Quarterly
- ○ Rarely or Never

APPENDIX 5

For the School or District Administrator, Coach Evaluation Form

The heart of instructional coaching is professional improvement that serves the best interests of students. This form describes key aspects of the role that research demonstrates have the greatest impact on students and schools.

1. The coach partners with teachers to gain a clear picture of reality in the classroom by analyzing one or more of the following forms of data: videorecording, student data, student interviews, and collecting classroom data at the request of the teacher. (Indicators 1.1 and 3.1)

    o   Always
    o   Frequently
    o   Sometimes
    o   Rarely or Never

2. The coach partners with teachers to identify clear, powerful, measurable, student-focused goals that are emotionally compelling for the teacher. (Indicators 1.2 and 3.2)

    o   Always
    o   Frequently
    o   Sometimes
    o   Rarely or Never

3. The coach uses the instructional playbook with high-impact strategies to offer teachers choices in strategies to use to hit their student-focused goals. (Indicator 1.3)

    o   Always
    o   Frequently
    o   Sometimes
    o   Rarely or Never

4. The coach uses checklists to describe clearly the teaching strategies that teachers choose to implement to hit their student-focused goals. (Indicator 1.4)

    o   Always
    o   Frequently

○ Sometimes

○ Rarely or Never

5. The coach encourages teachers to modify the strategies they use for their student-focused goals to meet student needs. (Indicator 1.4)

○ Always

○ Frequently

○ Sometimes

○ Rarely or Never

6. The coach models teaching strategies that assist teachers with understanding the strategies to meet their student-focused goals in one or more of the following ways: (Indicator 1.5)

» Teaching in the teacher's classroom

» Co-teaching in the teacher's classroom

» Before or after class (with no students in the room)
  Observing another teacher's classroom (with the coach)

» Observing another teacher's classroom (without the coach)

» Providing the teacher with video of a teacher using the strategy

○ Yes

○ No

7. The coach partners with teachers to problem solve and analyze goal progress until the goal is met. (Indicators 1.6, 1.7, 1.8, 1.9, and 3.3)

○ Always

○ Frequently

○ Sometimes

○ Rarely or Never

8. The coach treats all educators as partners and encourages dialogue over giving advice or directives. (Indicators 4.1 and 4.2)

- ○ Always
- ○ Frequently
- ○ Sometimes
- ○ Rarely or Never

9. The coach understands the complexities of working with adults and positions teachers as the primary decision-makers in the Impact Cycle. (Indicators 5.1 and 5.2)

- ○ Frequently
- ○ Rarely or Never

10. The coach has built trusting relationships with teachers that have led an increased number of teachers to be willing to work with the coach in Impact Cycles. (Indicator 6.1)

- ○ Always
- ○ Frequently
- ○ Sometimes
- ○ Rarely or Never

11. The coach shares instructional knowledge dialogically as a partner and not as an "expert" or as an evaluator. (Indicator 6.2)

- ○ Always
- ○ Frequently
- ○ Sometimes
- ○ Rarely or Never

12. The coach spends the following amount of work time on coaching cycles in which teachers set their own goals for students. (Indicators 7.1 and 7.2)

- ○ 70% or more
- ○ 50-69%
- ○ 30-49%
- ○ less than 30%

13. The coach communicates regularly with school and system leadership about coaching while maintaining confidentiality. (Indicators 7.1 and 7.2)

- ○ Weekly
- ○ Monthly
- ○ Quarterly
- ○ Rarely or Never

APPENDIX 6

The Impact Cycle Checklist

IDENTIFY	☑
Teacher gets a clear picture of current reality by watching a video of their lesson or by reviewing observation data (video is best!)	○
Coach asks the identify questions with the teacher to identify a goal	○
Teacher identifies a student-focused goal	○
Teacher identifies a teaching strategy to use to hit the goal	○

LEARN	☑
Coach shares a checklist for the chosen teaching strategy	○
Coach prompts the teacher to modify the practice if they wish	○
Teacher chooses an approach to modeling that they would like to observe and identifies a time to watch modeling	○
Coach provides modeling in one or more formats	○
Teacher sets a time to implement the practice	○

IMPROVE	☑
Teacher implements the practice	○
Data is gathered (by teacher or coach in class or while viewing video) on student progress toward to the goal	○
Data is gathered (by teacher or coach in class or while viewing video) on teacher's implementation of the practice (usually on the previously viewed checklist)	○
Coach and teacher meet to confirm direction and monitor progress	○
Coach and teacher make adaptations and plan next actions until the goal is met.	○

APPENDIX 7

Rubric for Instructional Coaching Programs

———

Adapted from the ICG Coaching Certification program (www. instructionalcoaching.com/certifications)

The coaching program demonstrates current, accomplished coaching practice around the Seven Success Factors for effective coaching programs (Knight, 2021).

PARTNERSHIP PRINCIPLES

No matter how much knowledge instructional coaches have, they will not be effective change leaders unless they understand the complexities of helping and working with adults. Instructional Coaching Programs demonstrate that their coaches understand how to interact with adults in ways that do not engender resistance.

QUALITY INDICATOR 1.1

Coaches use a dialogical approach (Knight, 2017) to coaching in which coaches and teachers are partners who use their collective strengths to make powerful classroom changes for students.

QUALITY INDICATOR 1.2

Coaches consistently embody the Partnership Principles (Knight, 2011) in coaching interactions to build trusting relationships with teachers and school and system leaders.

SCORE OF 1	SCORE OF 2	SCORE OF 3	SCORE OF 4
coaches do not work with teachers as partners	coaches unevenly work with teachers as partners	coaches consistently work with teachers as partners	coaches extensively work with teachers as partners
coaches minimally use a dialogical approach to coaching (Equality, Choice, Voice, and Reflection and Demonstrating Empathy, Listening, and Asking Better Questions)	coaches inconsistently use a dialogical approach to coaching (Equality, Choice, Voice, and Reflection and Demonstrating Empathy, Listening, and Asking Better Questions)	coaches often use a dialogical approach to coaching (Equality, Choice, Voice, and Reflection and Demonstrating Empathy, Listening, and Asking Better Questions)	coaches extensively use a dialogical approach to coaching (Equality, Choice, Voice, and Reflection and Demonstrating Empathy, Listening, and Asking Better Questions)
coaches do not share expertise with teachers positioned as the decision-makers	coaches inconsistently share expertise with teachers positioned as the decision-makers	coaches often share expertise with teachers positioned as the decision-makers	coaches effectively share expertise with teachers positioned as the decision-makers

coaches do not work with school and/or district leadership to clarify the theoretical basis of dialogical coaching so that coaches and leaders agree about what "instructional coaching" is	coaches infrequently work with school and/or district leadership to clarify the theoretical basis of dialogical coaching so that coaches and leaders agree about what "instructional coaching" is	coaches consistently work with school and/or district leadership to clarify the theoretical basis of dialogical coaching so that coaches and leaders agree about what "instructional coaching" is	coaches extensively work with school and/or district leadership to clarify the theoretical basis of dialogical coaching so that coaches and leaders agree about what "instructional coaching" is

STANDARD 2

THE IMPACT CYCLE

Instructional Coaching Programs effectively implement the Impact Cycle to partner with teachers in achieving their student-focused goals (Knight, 2017).

Identify

QUALITY INDICATOR 2.1

Coaches partner with teachers in obtaining a clear picture of current reality by using video, student interviews, student work, and/or observation data. [Current Reality]

QUALITY INDICATOR 2.2

Coaches use the Identify Questions with teachers to set a measurable student-focused goal. [Goal]

QUALITY INDICATOR 2.3

Coaches use an instructional playbook to aid teachers in choosing a high-impact teaching strategy to use to achieve their PEERS goals. [Strategy]

SCORE OF 1	SCORE OF 2	SCORE OF 3	SCORE OF 4
coaches ineffectively use the Identify Questions to set a goal for students	coaches partially or vaguely use the Identify Questions to set a goal for students	coaches effectively use the Identify Questions to set a goal for students	coaches insightfully use the Identify Questions to set a PEERS goal for students
teachers do not select the teaching strategy to achieve the goal and/or are not provided with an Instructional Playbook to use to choose a strategy	teachers select the teaching strategy to achieve the goal, but an Instructional Playbook is not provided	teachers select the teaching strategy to achieve the goal and are provided with an appropriate Instructional Playbook	teachers select the teaching strategy to achieve the goal by using a complete Instructional Playbook

Learn

QUALITY INDICATOR 2.4

Coaches use a checklist to explain the chosen teaching strategy to teachers and prompt teachers to modify the strategy as teachers wish. [Checklists]

QUALITY INDICATOR 2.5

Coaches model the strategy using a modeling approach that teachers have chosen. [Modeling]

SCORE OF 1	SCORE OF 2	SCORE OF 3	SCORE OF 4
coaches do not use a checklist to explain the teaching strategy that teachers have chosen to achieve the PEERS goal	coaches minimally use a checklist to explain the teaching strategy that teachers have chosen to achieve the PEERS goal	coaches consistently use a checklist to explain the teaching strategy that teachers have chosen to achieve the PEERS goal	coaches thoroughly and dialogically use a checklist to explain the teaching strategy that teachers have chosen to achieve the PEERS goal
coaches do not encourage teachers to modify the checklist according to student needs	coaches provide little encouragement for teachers to modify the checklist according to student needs	coaches encourage teachers to modify the checklist according to student needs	coaches significantly encourage teachers to modify the checklist according to student needs

coaches do not model the teaching strategy that teachers choose to achieve the PEERS goal and/or do not provide teachers with the six modeling options from which to choose	coaches minimally model the teaching strategy that teachers choose to achieve the PEERS goal and/or provide teachers with limited modeling options from which to choose	coaches effectively model the teaching strategy that teachers choose to achieve the PEERS goal and provide teachers with the six modeling options from which to choose	coaches thoroughly model the teaching strategy that teachers choose to achieve the PEERS goal and provide teachers with the six modeling options from which to choose

Improve

QUALITY INDICATOR 2.6

Coaches begin every coaching conversation by asking teachers about teachers' most pressing concerns. [Confirm Direction]

QUALITY INDICATOR 2.7

Coaches partner with teachers in gathering and analyzing data on student progress toward the PEERS goal. [Review Progress]

QUALITY INDICATOR 2.8

Coaches partner with teachers in making modifications until students achieve the PEERS goal. [Invent Improvements]

QUALITY INDICATOR 2.9

Coaches partner with teachers in determining more long-term work on goals as necessary or on future goals once goals are met. [Plan Next Actions]

SCORE OF 1	SCORE OF 2	SCORE OF 3	SCORE OF 4
coaches rarely begin coaching conversations by asking teachers about their most pressing concerns. [Confirm Direction]	coaches sometimes begin coaching conversations by asking teachers about their most pressing concerns. [Confirm Direction]	coaches often begin coaching conversations by asking teachers about their most pressing concerns. [Confirm Direction]	coaches always begin every coaching conversation by asking teachers about their most pressing concerns. [Confirm Direction]

coaches do not assist teachers in gathering and analyzing data on student progress toward goals [Review Progress]	coaches minimally assist teachers in gathering and analyzing data on student progress toward goals [Review Progress]	coaches effectively assist teachers in gathering and analyzing data on student progress toward goals [Review Progress]	coaches extensively support teachers in gathering and analyzing data on student progress toward goals [Review Progress]
coaches do not assist teachers in making modifications until students meet the goals [Invent Improvements]	coaches minimally assist teachers in making modifications until students meet the goals [Invent Improvements]	coaches effectively assist teachers in making modifications until students meet the goals [Invent Improvements]	coaches extensively support teachers in making modifications until students meet the goals [Invent Improvements]
coaches do not assist teachers in determining more long-term work on goals as necessary or on future goals once the goals are met [Plan Next Actions]	coaches minimally assist teachers in determining more long-term work on goals as necessary or on future goals once the goals are met [Plan Next Actions]	coaches effectively assist teachers in determining more long-term work on goals as necessary or on future goals once the goals are met [Plan Next Actions]	coaches extensively support teachers in determining more long-term work on goals as necessary or on future goals once the goals are met [Plan Next Actions]

STANDARD 3
DATA

Instructional Coaching Programs involve partnership with teachers to set PEERS goals and to monitor teachers' progress toward those goals, and that means that coaches must be able to gather and analyze data. (A description of the important data that coaches should gather and PEERS goals is included in Knight, 2017.)

QUALITY INDICATOR 3.1

Coaches partner with teachers in using video, student interviews, student work, and/or observation data in obtaining a clear picture of current reality in the classroom in an area of teacher-identified need.

QUALITY INDICATOR 3.2

Coaches partner with teachers in determining the form of measurement and appropriate data tools for a PEERS goal and how to track progress over time.

Coaches partner with teachers in gathering and analyzing data on the goal until students meet the goal.

SCORE OF 1	SCORE OF 2	SCORE OF 3	SCORE OF 4
coaches minimally analyze and/or use appropriate data (classroom video, student interviews, student work, and/or coach observation data) to help teachers get a clear picture of current reality and to choose a data-gathering process for the PEERS goal	coaches unevenly analyze and/or use appropriate data (classroom video, student interviews, student work, and/or coach observation data) to help teachers get a clear picture of current reality and to choose a data-gathering process for the PEERS goal	coaches often analyze and/or use appropriate data (classroom video, student interviews, student work, and/or coach observation data) to help teachers get a clear picture of current reality and to choose a data-gathering process for the PEERS goal	coaches extensively and insightfully analyze and/or use appropriate data (classroom video, student interviews, student work, and/or coach observation data) to help teachers get a clear picture of current reality and to choose a data-gathering process for the PEERS goal
coaches do not use appropriate data to help teachers get a clear picture of current reality	coaches minimally use appropriate data to help teachers get a clear picture of current reality	coaches effectively use appropriate data to help teachers get a clear picture of current reality	coaches extensively use appropriate data to help teachers get a clear picture of current reality
coaches do not help teachers in choosing a data-gathering process for the PEERS goal	coaches minimally assist teachers in choosing a data-gathering process for the PEERS goal	coaches assist teachers in choosing a data-gathering process for the PEERS goal	coaches significantly assist teachers in choosing a data-gathering process for the PEERS goal

STANDARD 4

INSTRUCTIONAL PLAYBOOK

Instructional Coaching Programs use an Instructional Playbook to partner with teachers to choose a strategy to achieve their PEERS goals. (See Knight, 2017, and Knight et al., 2020, for examples of instructional playbooks.)

QUALITY INDICATOR 4.1

Coaches create, maintain, and periodically update an instructional playbook tailored to the coaching audience that contains a selection of thoroughly vetted high-impact strategy choices for teachers to use to achieve their PEERS goals.

QUALITY INDICATOR 4.2

Coaches use the instructional playbook during the Identify Questions conversation to offer strategy choices to teachers.

QUALITY INDICATOR 4.3

The coaches' playbook contains a Table of Contents of instructional strategies, a One-Page Summary for each strategy on the Table of Contents, sufficient Checklists for each strategy, and an explanation of the coaching audience and how the playbook meets their current needs.

SCORE OF 1	SCORE OF 2	SCORE OF 3	SCORE OF 4
teachers do not select the teaching strategy to achieve the goal and/or is not provided with an Instructional Playbook to use to choose a strategy	teachers select the teaching strategy to achieve the goal, but an Instructional Playbook is not used	teachers select the teaching strategy to achieve the goal and are provided with an appropriate Instructional Playbook	teachers select the teaching strategy to achieve the goal by using a complete Instructional Playbook
the instructional playbook is incomplete or irrelevant and does not meets the needs of the coaching audience	the instructional playbook is incomplete and/or not clearly tied to the needs of the coaching audience	the instructional playbook is complete and minimally meets the needs of the coaching audience	the instructional playbook is complete and thoroughly meets the needs of the coaching audience

STANDARD 5

COMMUNICATION HABITS AND SKILLS

Because coaching involves communication, Instructional Coaching Programs continually engage coaches in improving their communication skills and in communicating about coaching with all school stakeholders to build a collaborative school culture.

QUALITY INDICATOR 5.1

Coaches communicate with teachers in a spirit of partnership as evidenced by use of the *Better Conversations* Habits (Demonstrating Empathy, Listening, Fostering Dialogue, Asking Better

Questions, Making Emotional Connections, Being a Witness to the Good, Finding Common Ground, Controlling Toxic Emotions, Redirecting Toxic Conversations, and Building Trust) as appropriate in coaching conversations (Knight, 2016).

QUALITY INDICATOR 5.2

Coaches communicate about the coaching role, the coaching approach, and the coaching process regularly with school and system administrators and teachers to foster a collaborative school culture.

SCORE OF 1	SCORE OF 2	SCORE OF 3	SCORE OF 4
coaches minimally use a dialogical approach to coaching (Equality, Choice, Voice, and Reflection and Demonstrating Empathy, Listening, and Asking Better Questions)	coaches inconsistently use a dialogical approach to coaching (Equality, Choice, Voice, and Reflection and Demonstrating Empathy, Listening, and Asking Better Questions)	coaches often use a dialogical approach to coaching (Equality, Choice, Voice, and Reflection and Demonstrating Empathy, Listening, and Asking Better Questions)	coaches extensively use a dialogical approach to coaching (Equality, Choice, Voice, and Reflection and Demonstrating Empathy, Listening, and Asking Better Questions)
coaches do not share expertise with teachers positioned as the decision-makers	coaches minimally share expertise with teachers positioned as the decision-makers	coaches consistently share expertise with teachers positioned as the decision-makers	coaches effectively share expertise with teachers and clearly position teachers as the decision-makers
COMMUNICATION			
coaches do not communicate about the coaching role regularly with school and system administrators and teachers	coaches minimally communicate about the coaching role with school and system administrators and teachers	coaches consistently communicate about the coaching role with school and system administrators and teachers	coaches extensively communicate about the coaching role with school and system administrators and teachers
coaches do not communicate about the coaching approach regularly with school and system administrators and teachers	coaches minimally communicate about the coaching approach with school and system administrators and teachers	coaches consistently communicate about the coaching approach with school and system administrators and teachers	coaches extensively communicate about the coaching approach with school and system administrators and teachers

coaches do not communicate about the coaching process with school and system administrators and teachers	coaches minimally communicate about the coaching process with school and system administrators and teachers	coaches consistently communicate about the coaching process with school and system administrators and teachers	coaches extensively communicate about the coaching process with school and system administrators and teachers
coaches do not help foster a collaborative school culture	coaches minimally foster a collaborative school culture	coaches consistently foster a collaborative school culture	coaches significantly foster a collaborative school culture

STANDARD 6

LEADERSHIP

Instructional Coaching Programs hire, develop, and support coaches who are emotionally intelligent, responsive to teachers, embody a stewardship approach during coaching, are ambitious for students, organized, and reliable (see Knight, 2016, chapter 9).

QUALITY INDICATOR 6.1

Coaches have built trusting relationships with teachers that have resulted in many teachers choosing to work with coaches in Impact Cycles.

QUALITY INDICATOR 6.2

Coaches have an exceptional level of instructional expertise and share that knowledge with teachers as appropriate but do so dialogically as partners, not as "experts" or as evaluators.

SCORE OF 1	SCORE OF 2	SCORE OF 3	SCORE OF 4
few teachers and/or an inconsistent number of teachers voluntarily choose to work with coaches	a small but consistent number of teachers voluntarily choose to work with coaches	an appropriate and growing number of teachers voluntarily choose to work with coaches	a significant and growing number of teachers voluntarily choose to work with coaches
coaches do not interact with teachers and leaders as partners	coaches inconsistently interact with teachers and leaders as partners	coaches consistently interact with teachers and leaders as partners	coaches extensively interact with teachers and leaders as partners and not as "experts"

SYSTEM SUPPORT

Instructional Coaching Programs flourish in systems that support them. When district leaders and, in particular, principals, support instructional coaching programs, effective coaches succeed. However, when support does not exist, effective coaches may have little or no impact (Knight, 2011).

QUALITY INDICATOR 7.1

Coaches have worked with school and/or district leadership to clarify the coaches' roles in the school, to clarify how the coaches should spend their time during the workday (with the majority of time spent working with teachers in Impact Cycles), to clarify the boundaries of confidentiality in coaching, and to communicate these policies and practices to teachers.

QUALITY INDICATOR 7.2

Coaches communicate regularly with school and/or district leadership to ensure that everyone who supports coaching views it with the same theoretical perspective and to address issues concerning the coaching role.

SCORE OF 1	SCORE OF 2	SCORE OF 3	SCORE OF 4
COMMUNICATION			
coaches do not communicate about the coaching role regularly with school and system administrators and teachers	coaches minimally communicate about the coaching role with school and system administrators and teachers	coaches consistently communicate about the coaching role with school and system administrators and teachers	coaches extensively communicate about the coaching role with school and system administrators and teachers
coaches do not communicate about the coaching approach regularly with school and system administrators and teachers	coaches minimally communicate about the coaching approach with school and system administrators and teachers	coaches consistently communicate about the coaching approach with school and system administrators and teachers	coaches extensively communicate about the coaching approach with school and system administrators and teachers
coaches do not communicate about the coaching process regularly with school and system administrators and teachers	coaches minimally communicate about the coaching process with school and system administrators and teachers	coaches consistently communicate about the coaching process with school and system administrators and teachers	coaches extensively communicate about the coaching process with school and system administrators and teachers
coaches do not help foster a collaborative school culture	coaches minimally foster a collaborative school culture	coaches consistently foster a collaborative school culture	coaches significantly foster a collaborative school culture
ROLE CLARITY / TIME			
coaches do not work with school and/or district leadership to clarify coaches' roles within the school	coaches minimally work with school and/or district leadership to clarify coaches' roles within the school	coaches consistently work with school and/or district leadership to clarify coaches' roles within the school	coaches extensively work with school and/or district leadership to clarify coaches' roles within the school
coaches do not work with school and/or district leadership to clarify how coaches should spend the time during the workday	coaches minimally work with school and/or district leadership to clarify how coaches should spend the time during the workday	coaches consistently work with school and/or district leadership to clarify how coaches should spend the time during the workday	coaches extensively work with school and/or district leadership to clarify how coaches should spend the time during the workday
coaches spend 1-25% of work time in Impact Cycles with teachers	coaches spend 26-45% of work time in Impact Cycles with teachers	coaches spend 46-59% of work time in Impact Cycles with teachers	coaches spend 60-100% of work time in Impact Cycles with teachers

CONFIDENTIALITY			
coaches do not work with school and/or district leadership to clarify the boundaries of confidentiality in coaching	coaches minimally work with school and/or district leadership to clarify the boundaries of confidentiality in coaching	coaches consistently work with school and/or district leadership to clarify the boundaries of confidentiality in coaching	coaches extensively work with school and/or district leadership to clarify the boundaries of confidentiality in coaching
coaches do not work with school and/or district leadership to clarify how to communicate confidentiality policies and practices to teachers	coaches infrequently work with school and/or district leadership to clarify how to communicate confidentiality policies and practices to teachers	coaches consistently work with school and/or district leadership to clarify how to communicate confidentiality policies and practices to teachers	coaches extensively work with school and/or district leadership to clarify how to communicate confidentiality policies and practices to teachers
PARTNERSHIP APPROACH			
coaches do not work with school and/or district leadership to clarify the theoretical basis of dialogical coaching so that coaches and leaders agree about what "instructional coaching" is	coaches infrequently work with school and/or district leadership to clarify the theoretical basis of dialogical coaching so that coaches and leaders agree about what "instructional coaching" is	coaches consistently work with school and/or district leadership to clarify the theoretical basis of dialogical coaching so that coaches and leaders agree about what "instructional coaching" is	coaches extensively work with school and/or district leadership to clarify the theoretical basis of dialogical coaching so that coaches and leaders agree about what "instructional coaching" is
coaches do not use a partnership approach in which coaches share expertise dialogically	coaches unevenly use a partnership approach in which coaches share expertise dialogically	coaches consistently embody a partnership approach in which coaches share expertise dialogically	coaches thoroughly embody a partnership approach in which coaches share expertise dialogically

Instructional Coach Candidate Evaluation Form

Candidate: _____

Evaluator: _____

Date: _____

Before using this scoring tool for candidates, the hiring manager and interview panel should meet to ensure

» Clear and consistent scoring understanding and practices among the team
» A deep analysis of potential scoring biases to eliminate bias in the hiring process
» Clarity on any differences in scoring for veteran coach candidates versus candidates who are new to coaching but are promising candidates

Evidence pieces in the hiring process to use in scoring:

» Candidate resumé
» Screening interview evidence
» Skills interview evidence
» Model interview evidence
» References interview evidence

SCORING KEY:

NOT RATED: Candidate is new to coaching and not able to demonstrate this element of the rubric

1: No experience/incompetent/does not meet expectations

2: Some experience/somewhat competent/could meet expectations

3: Experienced/competent/meets expectations

4: Very experienced/very competent/exceeds expectations

Based on the candidate's evidence pieces, place an "X" in the appropriate rating column.

INSTRUCTIONAL COACHING SUCCESS FACTOR	4	3	2	1	NOT RATED
PARTNERSHIP PRINCIPLES					
The candidate uses a dialogical approach to coaching in which the candidate and teachers are partners who use their collective strengths to make powerful classroom changes for students.					
The candidate consistently embodies the Partnership Principles in coaching interactions to build trusting relationships with teachers and school and system leaders.					
COMMENTS					
IMPACT CYCLE					
The candidate asks good questions to assist teachers in setting student-focused goals.					
The candidate uses an instructional playbook to aid the teacher in choosing a high-impact teaching strategy to use to achieve student-focused goals.					
The candidate skillfully explains teaching strategies.					
The candidate effectively models the use of instructional strategies.					
The candidate positions teachers as the decision-makers for their students.					
The candidate is flexible in making adjustments that meet student needs.					
COMMENTS					

DATA					
The candidate uses video, student interviews, student work, and/or observation data in obtaining a clear picture of current reality in the classroom.					
The candidate skillfully tracks goal data over time.					
The candidate gathers and analyzes data on student-focused goal until students meet the goal.					
COMMENTS					

INSTRUCTIONAL PLAYBOOK					
The candidate has a strong foundational knowledge of research-based instructional strategies.					
The coach uses the instructional playbook during the Identify Questions conversation to offer strategy choices to teachers.					
COMMENTS					

COMMUNICATION HABITS AND SKILLS					
The candidate communicates with teachers in a spirit of partnership as appropriate in coaching conversations.					
The candidate communicates about the coaching role, the coaching approach, and the coaching process regularly with school and system administrators and teachers to foster a collaborative school culture.					
COMMENTS					

LEADERSHIP					
The candidate has built trusting relationships with teachers.					

The candidate has an exceptional level of instructional expertise and shares that knowledge with teachers as appropriate but does so dialogically as a partner, not as an "expert" or as an evaluator.					
COMMENTS					

SYSTEM SUPPORT					
The candidate has worked with school and/or district leadership to clarify the coach's role in the school, to clarify how the coach should spend their time during the workday (with the majority of time spent working with teachers in Impact Cycles), to clarify the boundaries of confidentiality in coaching, and to communicate these policies and practices to teachers.					
The candidate communicates regularly with school and/or district leadership to ensure that everyone who supports coaching views it with the same theoretical perspective and to address issues concerning the coaching role.					
COMMENTS					
OTHER COACHING RESPONSIBILITIES					

INDEX

accountability, 5, 17

Administrator Feedback Form, 60, 262–266

adults, change and, 38–39

agency, goals and, 50

application information, qualifying hiring with, 142–143

assessment, evaluation vs., 35

audit process in program evaluation

    communication in the, 112–114

    content, developing, 103–104, 107–109

    data collection phase, 105–106

    insider vs. outsider evaluators, 110–111

    justifying the, 111

    leadership support, need for, 111–112

    Program Audit Development Form, 107–109

    transparency, 111–112

Better Conversations (Knight), 74–75

biographical data, qualifying hiring with, 142–143

change, 14, 18, 38–39, 193, 209

choice in partnered coaching, 40

clarity

    in evaluation, 13–16

    in hiring, 130, 136–137

    for retention, 204–205

Coach Candidate Evaluation Form, 174, 178, 283–287. See also job candidates

coaches

coaches for, xi, 213–214

    exceptional, attributes of, 37–38

    expectations limiting accomplishments of, 49

    misperceptions about, 37

    resistance to, overcoming, 38, 39

    training, benefits of, 191–192

    value as employees, 76, 195, 205–206, 208–209

coaches, effective

    characteristics of, 151–152, 156–157

    communication habits and skills of, 45–46, 234–235

    impacts of, 130

coaches, roles of

    all things to all people, 204

    as go-between, 112–114

    improvement specialists, 19

    instructional experts, 47

    interpretor, 113–114

    leadership through partnership, 46–47

    most common activities performed by, 48–49

    other duties as assigned, 14

    perceived, 36

    school improvement, 24

    supervisory, results of, 11–13

    teacher evaluators, 11–13

    variation in, 36

    vignette, 190–191

coach evaluation. See also 360-evaluation approach

    additional resources, 30

    aligned, purpose and process of, xx

annual, negative aspects of, 68

assessment vs., 35

best practices, benefits from, 6

data pieces most helpful for, 99–101

feedback in, 66–72

feedback vs., 67

human resources laws and policies for, 8,
13–16

Kirkpatrick model, 94

negative experiences, overcoming, 30

ongoing and timely, benefits of, 68

on performance, not on ratings for growth,
68–70

for positive change, 17–18, 30

process, 4–5, 8

purpose of, 8, 32

for retention, 19

sound, benefits of, 9–10

Sound Evaluation Checklist for, 10

Standards and Quality indicators for, 230–236

student-adult crossover in, 21

successful, 7, 13–21, 99–101

unclear and unaligned, results of, 6–7

using the beliefs and habits of Better Conversations, 72–76

vignettes, 4–5, 34–36

with intention and discretion, 70–72

without research-based standards, 17

without role-focused forms or rubrics, 5–6,
34–36

coach evaluation conversations

    difficult, avoiding, 66–67

    helpful, guidelines for, 67–68

    judgement in, 75

    partnership approach, 68, 73

    for performance interventions, 69

    providing a copy prior to, 69

Coach Evaluation Form, 262–266

coach evaluation forms

    Administrator Feedback Form, 262–266

    Administrator feedback Form, 60

    Coach Evaluation Form, 262–266

    Self-evaluation Form, 59–60, 256–260

    Teacher Feedback Form, 58–59, 250–254

coaching

    compulsory, results of, 12–13

    fostering a culture of, 49

    research-based definition of, 48

    resistance to, 38, 39

    term use, limitations of, 36

coaching champions, xi, 213–214

Coaching Feedback Form, 250–254

coaching practice, data collected on, 64–66

coach success

    aspirational markers of, 230–236

    plan elements supporting, 118

    system support in, xi, 47–49, 114–117, 235–236

coach success, requirements for

    communication habits and skills, x, 45–46,
234–235

    a conversational framework, x, 41–43, 231

    data collection, knowing about, x, 43–44

    high-impact instructional strategies, knowing
about, x, 44–45, 233–234

    a partnership approach, 40–41, 47, 48

    principles to guide actions, x

    principles to guide their actions, 40–41, 231

    professionalism, xi

    self-awareness, 47

    self-leadership and outward leadership skills,

x–xi, 46–47, 235

cognitive ability tests, qualifying hiring with, 143

communication audit process, 112–114

communication habits and skills

    improving, 74–76, 234–235

    in partnered coaching, 41

    quality indicators, 234–235

    rubric, 245–247, 277–279

    scoring job applicants on, 148–149

    to set goals, 75

    standard for effective programs, 45–46

    witnessing the good, 205

communication triangles, 112–114

conversation habits, improving, 75–76, 234–235

data

    for evaluation, 20–21, 70

    quality indicators, 233

    rubric, 243–244, 275–276

    standard for effective programs, 43–44

    sustaining professional learning programs, 94

data collection

    on coaching practice, 64–66

    for effective coaching programs, 43–44

    goal data, 63–64

    for program improvement, 214

    student data, 63–64

dialogue in partnered coaching, 41

emotional intelligence, 167

employees

    best performance, obtaining, 16–17

    dissatisfied, 199–200

    engaged, 198–200

    job satisfaction, predictors of, 197

equality in partnered coaching, 40

evaluation. See also 360-evaluation approach; coach evaluation

    annual, negative aspects of, 68

    feedback vs., 67

    ongoing and timely, benefits of, 68

    on performance, not on ratings for growth, 68–70

    using the beliefs and habits of Better Conversations, 72–76

    with intention and discretion, 70–72

evaluation conversations

    difficult, avoiding, 66–67

    helpful, guidelines for, 67–68

    judgement in, 75

    partnership approach, 68, 73

    for performance interventions, 69

    providing a copy prior to, 69

Fairfax County Public Schools rubric, 56–57

feedback

    additional resources, 82

    complexities of providing, 66–67

    concern-based, 71

    dialogical, 70

    evaluations vs., 67

    learning-based, 71–72

    negative, managing, 67, 71–72

    ongoing and timely, benefits of, 68

    on performance, not on ratings for growth, 68–70

    positive-based, 71–72

    360-evaluation approach, 51–52

    traditional, 69–70

    using the beliefs and habits of Better Conversations, 72–76

with intention and discretion, 70–72

feedback conversations

difficult, avoiding, 66–67

helpful, guidelines for, 67–68

judgement in, 75

partnership approach, 68, 73

for performance interventions, 69

providing a copy prior to, 69

feedback forms

Administrator Feedback Form, 60

Coaching Feedback Form, 250–254

Teacher Feedback Form, 250–254

Teacher feedback Form, 58–59

goals

achieving, strategies for, 43–44

aspirational, 50–51

hope and, 50

learning and, 15

goal-setting

for academic achievement, 63

for classroom management, 63

conversation habits for, 75

data collection for, 43–44

for engagement, 63

Identify Questions for, 44

for improvement, 50–51

PEERS goals, 63–64, 100–101

for positive learning environments, 63

GROWTH Coaching, 70–71

habits in conversation, improving, 75–76, 234–235

hiring coaches

the best, persistent beliefs surrounding, 151

changes, post-WW II, 132–133

human resources role in, 138

justifying, 5

Planning for Recruiting and Hiring Coaches Checklist, 135–136

rubric for, 178–179, 283–287

standards, 134–137

successful, 151

system support element, 115–116

using evaluation tools in the, 143, 145

vignette, 128–130, 190

hiring interview

additional resources, 186

authentic responses in, 159

bias in, 160, 161–163, 178, 186

format for the, 163

as interrogation, avoiding, 174

judgement, withholding, 174

legal considerations, 165–166

the model interview, 164–165, 171–173

planning for, 173–174

problems, avoiding, 160–161

qualifying for hiring in, 142–143

the references interview, 165

the screening interview, 163–164, 166–167

the skills interview, 164, 167–171

structured approach, 163

hiring interview questions

behavioral and competency-based, 168

choosing the, 165

to clarify skills and experience, 166

continuous improvement of, 175–178

for emotional intelligence, 167

on meeting non-negotiable aspects, 166

the model interview, 171–173

relevant, 159–160

sample, 175–177

scenario-based, 171

the screening interview, 166–167

situational, 168–169

the skills interview, 167–171

hiring interview team

choosing the, 160–161

in interview planning, 173–174

to reduce bias, 161–163

hiring process. See also job candidates

making the decision, 178–180

overview, 126

technology in the, 133

hiring process, job description in the

expectations in the, 141–143

one-page scorecard informing, 140–145

for retention, 204–205

salary information, 140

sample items, 138–140

setting standards for the, 136–137

specifying what is not in the, 140

using evaluation tools to develop the, 137–138

hiring qualifications, evidence used to show

application information, 142–143

biographical data, 142–143

cognitive ability tests, 143

interviews, 142

physical ability tests, 143

references, 142–143

work samples, 143

hope, requirements for, 50

ICG Coaching Certification process, 55–57, 101

ICG Coaching Certification rubrics, 102

ICG Coaching model, 38–39

identify phase of the Impact Cycle, 42, 44, 48, 231–232

identify phase of the Impact Cycle Checklist, 269

impact, data measuring

coaching practice, 64–66

goal data for, 64

PEERS goals achieved, 99–101

purpose of, 62–63

student data, 63–64

Impact Cycle. See also specific phases

defined, x

PEERS goals, 63–64, 99–101

quality indicators, 231–232

rubric, 240–243, 272–273

sample items for job descriptions, 138–140

standard for effective programs, 41–43

Impact Cycle Checklist, 64, 268–269

Impact Cycle coaching, 49, 63–64, 137

Impact Schools, 92

improve phase of the Impact Cycle, 42–43, 48, 232–233, 242–243, 274–275

improve phase of the Impact Cycle Checklist, 269

inside out professional development, viii–ix

insider evaluators, 110–111

Instructional Coach Rubric, 238–239

Instructional Playbook

to achieve student goals, x, 44–45

quality indicators, 233–234

rubric, 244–245, 276–277

standard for effective programs, 44–45

instructional strategies, high-impact. See Instructional Playbook

job candidate qualifications

application information, 142–143

biographical data, 142–143

cognitive ability tests, 143

interviews, 142

physical ability tests, 143

references, 142–143

work samples, 143

job candidates

authentic responses from, 159

Coach Candidate Evaluation Form, 174, 178, 283–287

culture fit, 160

hiring the best, 158–161, 178–180

internal vs. external, 152–154

managing the experience of, 157–158

role clarity for, 130, 136–137

job candidates, scoring

communication habits and skills, 148–149, 234–235

leadership, 150–151, 235

Partnership Principles, 146–147

job description in the hiring process

expectations in the, 141–143

one-page scorecard informing, 140–145

for retention, 204–205

salary information, 140

sample items, 138–140

setting standards for the, 136–137

specifying what is not in the, 140

using evaluation tools to develop the, 137–138

leadership

to develop professional culture, 212

quality indicators, 235

rubric, 247–248, 279–280

scoring job applicants on, 148–149

standard for effective programs, 46–47

supporting the audit process, 111–112

learning

by adults vs. children, 136

deep and sustainable, 14–15

goals and, 15

in partnership, 41

learning in action, 14

learn phase of the Impact Cycle, 42, 48, 232, 241–242, 273–274

learn phase of the Impact Cycle Checklist, 269

model interview, 164–165, 171–173

No Child Left Behind (NCLB) Act, 2–3

organizational change, 17–18

outside in professional development, viii–ix

outsider evaluators, 110–111

Partnership Principles

choice, 40

defined, x

dialogue, 41, 47

equality, 40

praxis, 41

quality indicators, 231

reciprocity, 41

reflection, 40–41

rubric, 239–240, 271–272

scoring job applicants on, 146–147

standard for effective programs, 40–41

voice, 40

PEERS goals, 63–64, 99–101

physical ability tests, qualifying hiring with, 143

Planning a Coaching Program Evaluation Process Checklist, 92

praxis in partnered coaching, 41

professional development
  defined, 88
  outside in/inside out, viii–ix
  professional learning vs., 88
  resistance to, ix

professional learning
  characteristics of in Impact Schools, 92
  defined, 88
  evaluating, 90, 93–94
  professional development vs., 88
  in school improvement, 90

professional learning experiences, four facets of, 93

professional learning programs, 90–91, 94

Program Audit Development Form, 107–109

program evaluation
  additional resources, 101, 124
  clarity, importance in, 13–16
  coach evaluation process informing, 98–99, 101–102
  forms of evidence in, 99–101, 275–276
  leadership, 279–280
  mistakes made when, 91
  objective, 99
  Planning a Coaching Program Evaluation Process Checklist, 92
  process, 6, 89, 91–92
  Program Evaluation Development Form, 103–104
  purpose of, 10–11, 84, 89

Reason to Evaluate Coaching Programs Checklist, 11

Seven Success Factors framework, 97–98

system support in, 280–282

program evaluation audit process
  communication in the, 112–114
  content, developing the, 103–104, 107–109
  data collection phase, 105–106
  insider vs. outsider evaluators, 110–111
  justifying the, 111
  leadership support, need for, 111–112
  Program Audit Development Form, 107–109
  transparency, 111–112

Program Evaluation Development Form, 103–104

program evaluation rubrics
  communication habits and skills, 277–279
  data, 275–276
  Impact Cycle, 272–273
  Instructional Playbook, 276–277
  leadership, 279–280
  Partnership Principles, 271–272
  system support, 280–282

program evaluation tools, creating
  compare Standards and Quality indicators to what coaches do, 98, 103
  determine data types and evidence demonstrating performance, 98–101, 103–104
  Standards and Quality indicators for, 97–98, 103, 230–236
  use data to make judgments about performance and to shape goals for improvement, 102–105

programs
  effectiveness, measuring, 5
  implementation vignette, 86–88

implementing without research, 13–14

program success

aspirational markers of, 230–236

evidence of, 87–89, 99–101

program success, standards for

communication habits and skills, x, 45–46, 234–235

data, x, 43–44

Impact Cycle, x, 41–43, 48, 231–232

Instructional Playbook, x, 44–45, 233–234

leadership, x–xi, 46–47, 235

Partnership Principles, x, 40–41, 231

system support, xi, 47–49

progression of withdrawal theory, 199–200

Race to the Top (DOE), 3

Reason to Evaluate Coaching Programs Checklist, 11

reciprocity in partnered coaching, 41

recruiting

focused on coaching not promotion, 156–157

human resources role in, 152, 157–158

internal vs. external, 152–154

passive vs. active job seekers, 133, 155–156

Planning for Recruiting and Hiring Coaches Checklist, 135–136

technology in, 133

references, qualifying hiring with, 142–143

references interview, 165

reflection in partnered coaching, 40–41

retention

additional resources, 220

coach-supervisor relationships in, 203–204, 207–208

collaboration and support in, 201–204

communicating value for, 205–206, 208–209

compensation and rewards, 205–206

engagement in, 198–204

fairness, perceptions of, 207

managing for, 196

process, 188

professional development for, 207–208

recruiting for, 204–205

Retaining Coaches and Sustaining Programs Checklists, 194–195

role clarity for, 204–205

socialization opportunities in, 201

supervision, impact on, 206–207

teacher, 92–93

retention plans

checklist, 194

developing, 198, 208–209

emphasizing engagement, 198–200

importance of, 194–195

rubrics, purpose of, 21

school improvement, 6, 90

school reform movements, 2–4

school staffing, percent of budgets spent on, 5

screening interview, 163–164, 166–167

Self-evaluation Form, 59–60, 256–260

skills interview, 164, 167–171

Sound Evaluation Checklist, 10

Standards and Quality indicators for Instructional Coaches, 230–236

Standards Movement, 2

supervisor, defined, 11–12

sustainability, program

additional resources, 220

evaluation for improvement, 214–215

planning for, 195, 209–211

process, 188

professional culture in, 211–212

Retaining Coaches and Sustaining Programs
Checklists, 194–195

supporting coaching champions and, 213–214

threats to, 6, 88–89, 192

without metrics, 6, 88–89

system support

in coach success, xi, 47–49, 114–117, 235–236

in hiring, 115–116

key areas of, 115–117, 130

in program evaluation, 280–282

program success and, xi, 47–49

quality indicators, 235–236

rubric, 248–249, 280–282

standard for effective programs, 47–49

teacher-coach relationships

building, 46–47, 154–155

hope component in, 50

internal hires, effect on, 154

in overcoming resistance, 38, 39

trusting, factors in, 156

Teacher Feedback Form, 58–59, 250–254

teachers

evaluation by coaches, results of, 11–13

psychic rewards for, 92–93

reforming evaluation of, 3–4

retaining, 92–93

teachers on special assignment (TOSAs), 5–6

teaching, parent-child dynamic in, 37–38

teams, effective, 211–212

360-evaluation approach

additional resources, 82

implementing, 82

overview, 51–55

360-evaluation approach, evidence from the

data collected from teachers, 58–59

data collected on coaching practice, 64–66

data collected on students, 63–64

purpose of requirement for, 62–63

360-evaluation approach, forms aligned with
standards

Administrator Feedback Form, 60, 262–266

modifying the, 61–63

Self-evaluation Form, 59–60, 256–260

Teacher Feedback Form, 58–59, 250–254

360-evaluation approach, tools

checklist, 54

development of the, 55–56

rubrics, 56–57, 238–239

360-Evaluation Process for Coaches Checklist, 54

training, change and, 17

turnover, 196–197

voice in partnered coaching, 40

work samples, qualifying hiring with, 143